# Making the Most of Meetings

## A Practical Guide

*Paula Jorde Bloom*

# NEW HORIZONS

EDUCATIONAL CONSULTANTS AND LEARNING RESOURCES

LAKE FOREST, ILLINOIS 60045-0863

Printed in the United States of America

**Library of Congress Cataloging-in-Publication Data**

Bloom, Paula Jorde, 1947-
    Making the Most of Meetings: a practical guide /
Paula Jorde Bloom. — 1st ed.
    p. cm. — (The director's toolbox: a
management series for early childhood
administrators)
    Includes bibliographical references.
    LCCN: 2002101428
    ISBN: 0-9621894-5-6


    1. Early childhood education—Administration.
2. Meetings—Planning.   I. Title.   II. Series

LB2822.6.B56 2002              372.21
                              QBI02-200163

# NEW HORIZONS

Educational Consultants and Learning Resources
P.O. Box 863
Lake Forest, Illinois 60045-0863
(847) 295-8131
(847) 295-2968 FAX

Books in **The Director's Toolbox Management Series** are available at quantity discounts for use in training programs. For information on bulk quantity rates or how to purchase a **Trainer's Guide** for this book, contact the publisher.

***Illustrations*** – *Marc Bermann*
***Design*** – *Stan Burkat*

# CONTENTS

# Chapter

# About the Author

Paula Jorde Bloom holds a joint appointment as Director of the Center for Early Childhood Leadership and Professor of Early Childhood Education at National-Louis University in Wheeling, Illinois. She received her baccalaureate degree from Southern Connecticut State University and her master's and Ph.D. degrees from Stanford University. Dr. Bloom has taught preschool and kindergarten, designed and directed a child care center, and served as administrator of a campus laboratory school. She is a frequent keynote speaker at state, national, and international early childhood conferences and serves as consultant to professional organizations and state agencies. Paula is the author of numerous articles and several widely read books including Workshop Essentials, Circle of Influence, Living and Learning with Children, Avoiding Burnout, A Great Place to Work, and Blueprint for Action.

# Acknowledgements

Like you, I've sat through hundreds of meetings, some stimulating and inspiring, others dreary and insufferable. But each one, good or bad, has served as a rich source of material for this book. I am grateful to my colleagues at the Center for Early Childhood Leadership for many of the lessons I've learned about effective meeting facilitation. Our monthly meetings serve as a wonderful laboratory for trying out new ideas and techniques.

In writing this book, I received helpful suggestions from Jill Bella, Eileen Eisenberg, Lila Goldston, Janis Jones, Judy Harris Helm, Cindy Mahr, Karen Points, and Teri Talan. Thanks also to Heather Knapp for tracking down several references and to Tim Walker and Catherine Cauman for their careful editing of the manuscript.

## CHAPTER 1

# Let's Get
# Together for a Meeting

*You dread the announcement. A mandatory meeting you can't avoid. You do not want to go, but your presence is expected. You get a nauseated feeling in the pit of your stomach just thinking about the meeting because you know what is in store— an agenda that lacks focus, a litany of boring announcements, rambling and disjointed discussions on topics that do not pertain to you, distracting interruptions, and group decisions that will go nowhere. Halfway through the meeting, you start to fidget and sneak a peek at your watch to see how many more minutes of tedium you have to bear. You are annoyed because you have so many more pressing things to do—even cleaning the gerbil cage and sorting broken crayons seem like great alternatives. By the time the meeting is over, though, you are no longer annoyed; you are angry. Angry because you realize that another opportunity has slipped by—an opportunity for learning, feeling valued, and engaging in substantive conversation and problem solving. Such a waste of time. Such a waste of human resources.*

There are few experiences in the world of work that virtually all adults can say they have in common, but suffering through a boring meeting may well be one of them. To be sure, the settings are different—plush boardroom in the corporate headquarters versus child-size chairs and the smell of disinfectant in the early childhood center—but the elements are essentially the same. You've been there no doubt.

## Meetings, Meetings, and More Meetings

Meetings are the glue that holds organizations together. Early childhood organizations are no exception. Whether it is a weekly staff meeting, a monthly parent meeting, or an annual board meeting, administrators of early childhood programs rely on meetings as the primary vehicle for communicating information, identifying and solving problems, and making new decisions and modifying old ones. Meetings are a great forum for creating team spirit and celebrating success. When planned and conducted well, meetings can be the director's most powerful tool for tapping the creative energy of staff and fostering greater commitment to shared goals. If run poorly, however, meetings are a waste of time, a waste of dollars, and a source of resentment among staff.

Technically defined, a meeting is any informal or formal gathering of three or more individuals with an expressed intent to share information, solve problems, plan events, or promote professional development. Meetings are essential because groups can usually generate more ideas, make bolder plans, and come up with wiser decisions than can individuals working alone. Meetings are simply the best venue administrators have for harnessing the collective creativity of the staff and sparking the synergy needed to increase the effectiveness of a center.

When done right, meetings are more than just a vehicle for solving problems; they can be enriching opportunities to support learning and strengthen interpersonal understanding and connections. Meetings fulfill our need to belong, to be affiliated with others. The face-to-face exchanges in a meeting environment provide us with immediate feedback of others' reactions to our ideas.

Given that meetings are essential for smooth program functioning and for a unified team approach, it is unfortunate that in many early childhood programs, poorly run meetings are the norm rather than the exception. They are viewed as something to be endured—a time when nothing is accomplished and people end up feeling frustrated, bored, or even resentful.

## Some Things Meetings Can and Can't Do

### Meetings can't...

- make reluctant decision makers decisive and bold.
- turn bored, unproductive workers into motivated, high achievers.
- take the place of individual planning and goal setting.

### Meetings can...

- bring together people with divergent viewpoints to discuss issues, air differences, and resolve conflicts.
- disseminate information to fairly large groups, with the opportunity for on-the-spot questions, explanations, and feedback.
- create a participative work environment through encouragement and sincere consideration of ideas, suggestions, and complaints from all segments of the organization.
- help administrators keep track of the status of projects and day-to-day activities and progress toward previously set goals.
- facilitate decision making by gathering all available data and selecting from among alternatives.
- focus a group's attention on a specific problem for immediate resolution.

*Adapted from Hamann, J. A. (1984). How to avoid BORED meetings. Madison: University of Wisconsin Press.*

A recent study conducted by the Center for Early Childhood Leadership at National-Louis University assessed early childhood practitioners' perceptions about meetings. The 450 respondents indicated that 20% of their time spent in meetings is unproductive and wasted. They considered less than half the time in meetings to be highly productive and an excellent use of their time.

Consider the implications of these findings. Directors report that they spend on average six hours each week in different types of professional meetings. Over the span of a career, that's more than 7,800 hours of professional life spent in meetings. If one-fifth of that time is perceived as unproductive and wasted, what does that portend for the overall job satisfaction and fulfillment of the early childhood workforce?

## How Much Time Do You Spend in Meetings?

Take a minute to think about the meetings you as an early childhood professional attend on a regular or occasional basis. Some meetings occur only quarterly; others more often. To get a sense of how much time you spend in meetings each week, calculate using the total number of hours per month you spend in different types of meetings.

**exercise 1**

| Type of Meeting | Hours/Month |
|---|---|
| Work-group team meetings | |
| Centerwide staff meetings | |
| Parent meetings | |
| Sponsoring agency meetings | |
| Board meetings | |
| Union meetings | |
| Professional organization meetings | |
| Other early childhood meetings | |

Looking at the big picture—all the meetings you attend each month—divide the total by 4 to calculate the average number of hours a week you spend in meetings:

_____ hours a week

Evaluate the meetings you attend in terms of your personal investment of time. What percentage of your meetings would fit in each of the categories below? *(The total should add up to 100%)*

_____ % Unproductive, a waste of time
_____ % Somewhat productive, a good use of time
_____ % Highly productive, an excellent use of time

One of the great things an organization can do is to help people give voice to their dreams, and provide the means by which people come together to create something greater than themselves.

*James Champy*

3

## What Bugs You Most About Meetings?

Now think about all those meetings you attend—how they are planned, how they are conducted, and the specific elements of the group process that takes place. What bugs you most about meetings? In the following exercise, indicate what you believe are the most common problems keeping meetings from being more productive. Feel free to add an item or two if you think of something not included on the list:

**exercise 2**

- ❑ An agenda is not distributed beforehand, so people don't know what to expect.
- ❑ The agenda is too ambitious; too much to cover in the time allotted.
- ❑ Participation is not balanced. Some people dominate the discussion.
- ❑ The group does not stay on task; it jumps from one topic to another.
- ❑ People talk at the same time and don't listen to each other.
- ❑ People are reluctant to express their true feelings.
- ❑ Meetings don't start on time and/or they don't end on time.
- ❑ People often arrive late and/or leave early.
- ❑ Decisions are often vague and it is unclear who is to carry them out.
- ❑ There is insufficient follow through after the meeting.
- ❑ No one takes minutes, so there is no accurate record of the meeting.
- ❑ _____
- ❑ _____

## Mary, Mary, Quite Contrary... What Do Your Meetings Cost?

Investing some time to improve your meetings makes good business sense when you consider of the financial implications of hosting a gathering of busy people with important jobs to do. Exercise 3 provides a simple formula to give you a sense of the real cost of bringing people together. This total doesn't even factor in the time you spend as the convener planning your meeting or the reimbursable expenses for travel, parking, photocopying, room rental, or refreshments.

1. Name a typical weekly or monthly meeting you convene: _____

2. How much time will each participant spend preparing for this meeting? _____ hour(s)

3. How long does the meeting run? _____ hours

4. Add individual preparation time (#2) and meeting length (#3): _____ hours

5. How many participants will be attending this meeting? _____ participants

6. Multiply total time (#4) by number of participants (#5): _____

7. Estimate the average hourly wage of the participants: $_____

8. Multiply #6 by #7: $ _____ **is the estimated cost of the meeting**

## Example

1. Name a typical weekly or monthly meeting you convene: _monthly staff meeting_

2. How much time will each participant spend preparing for this meeting? __1/2__ hour(s)

3. How long does the meeting run? __2 1/2__ hours

4. Add individual preparation time (#2) and meeting length (#3): ___3___ hours

5. How many participants will be attending this meeting? __18__ participants

6. Multiply total time (#4) by number of participants (#5): __54__

7. Estimate the average hourly wage of the participants: $__12.00__

8. Multiply #6 by #7: $ ___648.00___ **is the estimated cost of the meeting**

## Conditions for Success

Meetings don't have to be unproductive and frustrating. There are specific methods administrators can use to plan and conduct successful meetings. The skills involved take patience and practice to acquire, but the payoff is well worth it. Simply put, well-run meetings can have a remarkable effect on the degree of cohesion binding individuals together and the spirit in which those individuals relate to one another.

Running a successful meeting is both an art and a science. It is an art in that you must have a keen awareness of how to balance the task and the process. The **task** is the work to be done—the information to be communicated, the problems to be discussed, and the decisions to be made. The **process** is how the task is accomplished—how the decisions are made and the ways in which participants are empowered to be fully engaged in the deliberations. It is a science in that you can learn technical skills to help you achieve your goals—planning a meaningful agenda, establishing a conducive environment, asking effective questions, and giving clear, concise feedback. In a nutshell, here are the conditions for a successful meeting.

**The meeting has a purpose.** Every meeting needs a clearly stated purpose, a reason for being convened. The purpose needs to be communicated to the participants before the meeting and again during the leader's opening remarks.

**The agenda is distributed to participants prior to the meeting.** An agenda serves as a road map for a meeting. It alerts people to the topics that will be covered, the importance of each topic, and the time allocated to each topic. An agenda communicates essential information about the different roles people will play and the issues that participants should think about, bring, or read beforehand.

**The content meets the needs of attendees.** Careful thought is given to who should be invited to the meeting. Only people with vital interest in the substance of the meeting should attend. The content needs to be relevant and meaningful for people to believe that their time in the meeting is well spent.

**Time is managed carefully.** Conducting meetings successfully means that you begin and end them on time, showing respect for the participants and their busy lives. Time is orchestrated carefully during the meeting as well, so the content is covered yet everyone has an opportunity to be heard.

**Participation is balanced.** The processes of a meeting are just as crucial as the content. People need to be fully engaged and free to express their opinions without being allowed to dominate the discussion or sidetrack the focus of the meeting, thereby preventing the group from completing its work.

**The meeting provides closure**. A meeting culminates with a clear summary of what has been accomplished, the actions that need to take place afterward, and the roles and responsibilities of the participants. Informal or formal opportunities to evaluate the meeting's effectiveness also contribute to closure.

## Evaluating Your Meetings

Managing meetings effectively is one of the most important and challenging administrative responsibilities of early childhood directors. It is a dynamic process because contexts change, people change, and issues change. If you are to harness the potential power of meetings, you too must be flexible and change. This book is designed to help you do that.

*Making the Most of Meetings* is a no-nonsense, practical guide to reversing the slump you may be experiencing in meeting effectiveness. The topics covered will help you accomplish more in the meetings you plan and conduct. You'll learn how to increase participants' commitment to shared goals, arrive at decisions supported by everyone, and have more fun in the process.

No doubt about it, making the most of your meetings takes time. There is a big difference between understanding how to make meetings work and actually putting those principles into practice. I hope this book will help you achieve both.

Before we jump into action detailing the specifics of how to plan and conduct more effective meetings, take a moment to reflect on the meetings you convene and facilitate as you complete Exercise 4.

## exercise 4

Think about a recent meeting that you convened and in which you served as facilitator. The following items will help you evaluate your preparation for that meeting and the group dynamic and processes used during the meeting.

❑ I distributed the agenda prior to the meeting.

❑ Participants had an opportunity to contribute to the agenda.

❑ I gave sufficient advance notice about the meeting to ensure high attendance.

☐ The topics were relevant to the participants attending.

❑ Sufficient time was allotted for each topic.

❑ The meeting room was ample given the size of the group.

❑ The chairs were comfortable (adult-size) and a writing surface was provided.

❑ The location was free from distracting noises and interruptions.

❑ The meeting began on time.

❑ Discussion stayed on track and time was monitored.

❑ The tone of the meeting was cordial yet professional.

❑ Everyone had an opportunity to express his or her opinion on topics.

❑ Participants listened respectfully to one another.

❑ No one dominated the discussion.

❑ I periodically summarized the group's progress during the meeting.

❑ I summarized the group's accomplishments at the end of the meeting.

❑ Follow-up responsibilities were decided and agreed upon.

❑ Everyone stayed until the end of the meeting.

❑ The meeting ended on time.

❑ Minutes of the meeting were distributed to all attendees afterward.

# CHAPTER 2

# Anatomy of a Meeting

If we did a quick word association for the term *meeting*, no doubt you'd think of *Robert's Rules of Order* and the student government meetings you attended in junior high school. True, most meetings have their roots in some version of parliamentary procedure. The leader or chair sits at the head of the table overseeing the flow of discussion and actions taken by members. The secretary, elected by the group, dutifully takes minutes, recording old business, new business, resolutions made, and all the ayes and nays of the day.

*Robert's Rules of Order* may be appropriate for meetings conducted around formal debate and win/lose decision making. Indeed, many governmental bodies, including Congress, city councils, and local school boards, rely on parliamentary procedure to provide order to their proceedings. *Roberts Rules of Order* may also be useful for large groups where the topic is controversial and maintaining order is paramount, or for formal board meetings governed by bylaws. The rules are not conducive, however, to a collegial atmosphere in which to generate new ideas, analyze problems, and develop collaborative strategies for action. In other words, if you want to lead meetings that encourage collaboration, foster cohesiveness, and promote consensus decision making, put your copy of *Robert's* back on your bookshelf and adopt less formal meeting processes like those described in the following chapters.

## Dissecting the Whole

To plan and conduct an effective meeting, it is important to first understand the essential elements of the event. We can dissect a meeting into four parts.

**Content.** The content is what you want to accomplish, the topics of discussion, the information to be imparted, the data to be analyzed, and the knowledge, experience, and opinions the participants bring to the table.

**Structure.** The structure of a meeting includes the day and time it is held, the location, the management of the physical environment, whether or not there is an agenda, the order of topics to be considered, and the time allocated to each topic. Think of structure as the way the content is organized.

**Processes.** Meeting processes include how leadership is exercised, how discussion is carried out, how decisions are made, and how sensitive or contentious issues are handled. In other words, meeting processes focus on interpersonal interactions during the meeting and how the group functions as a whole.

**Culture.** The culture of a meeting is the climate or atmosphere of the event and the psychological investment of the participants. Are the proceedings friendly or divisive, cooperative or competitive, informal or formal, open or closed, trusting or adversarial? The culture is strongly influenced by the history of the group and the organization.

## Types of Meetings

Naomi is the director of a community-based nonprofit child care center serving infants and toddlers, preschoolers, and school-age children. She attends numerous meetings every month, each intended to accomplish different things. Here is a sample of the meetings Naomi attended during a recent month.

- Biweekly staff meetings with the center's 22 teachers and support staff. Naomi convenes these meetings and serves as facilitator. Topics include planning for upcoming events, sharing resources, disseminating information, and making decisions about centerwide issues of concern.

- A meeting with the city's zoning commission to talk about the impact of scheduled road construction on the center's traffic flow. At this meeting Naomi was an invited guest providing data and information.

- A meeting with the center's four lead teachers to discuss ways to improve child assessment procedures. Naomi convened this meeting and served as facilitator.

- A meeting with the kindergarten teachers at a nearby elementary school to talk about school readiness expectations. The principal of the elementary school convened this meeting and invited Naomi. The goal was to establish an ongoing relationship between the center and the school regarding kindergarten transitions.

- A meeting with the center's school-age care team to talk about the behavior of a child in the after-school program who bullies younger children in the group. The goal of the meeting was to come up with an intervention plan to strengthen the child's prosocial behaviors.

- A planning meeting for the executive board of the Greater Metro Early Childhood Directors Council. Naomi serves as secretary on the council. The executive board meets prior to the bimonthly meetings to develop an agenda, plan future speakers, and talk about fundraising. At the executive board meetings and the bimonthly meetings, Naomi serves as recorder and writes up the minutes.

- An early childhood department meeting at the local community college. Naomi teaches a class at the community college each semester, so she is invited to attend these monthly meetings.

- A centerwide staff development meeting to introduce the Work Sampling System. Naomi and her lead teachers planned the agenda for this meeting together. Naomi invited the students from her community college class to attend as well. Total attendance was 45. Naomi took the lead in preparing the agenda and inviting the speaker. Her lead teachers planned refreshments and prepared handouts.

- A meeting conducted by the state's Department of Children's Services to review new licensing guidelines for infant-toddler programs. Naomi was one of 25 attendees at this meeting.

- A Parent Advisory Board meeting to plan the spring fundraising event. Naomi worked with the president of the Parent Advisory Board to plan the agenda for this meeting. The president of the board facilitates the meetings.

- A meeting with the local T.E.A.C.H. coordinator and seven teachers. Naomi convened this meeting and served as facilitator. The purpose was to share information about the T.E.A.C.H. scholarship program and invite the teachers' participation.

No doubt about it, Naomi is one busy lady. She spends many hours every month attending meetings—some that she convenes, others where she serves as recorder, and others where she is a participant. The variety of meetings she attends will resonate with any early childhood administrator. While these meetings seem quite diverse, they can be grouped into four general categories: informational, professional development, problem solving, and planning. Some, if not most, of the meetings early childhood educators attend serve multiple purposes and fit into more than one category.

**Informational.** As the name implies, informational meetings are intended to transmit information—information about policies, procedures, people, and events. While informational meetings are typically structured as one-way communication, many also include opportunities for participants to ask questions or provide feedback about the information being shared.

> The meeting Naomi attended at the Department of Children's Services is an example of an informational meeting. For 45 minutes of the hour-long meeting the department's field liaison walked the participants through changes in the licensing code. The last 15 minutes were reserved for questions and answers about the new regulations.

**Professional development.** While similar to informational meetings, professional development meetings do more than merely transmit information. In addition to increasing participants' knowledge base about an issue or topic, professional development meetings also seek to change the behavior and attitudes of participants in an effort to increase their professional competence.

> At one of her recent staff meetings, Naomi invited a Red Cross volunteer to demonstrate CPR, the Heimlich maneuver, and other first-aid procedures. Her staff then took time to practice the techniques and talk about how and when they might use them. This discussion led into a broader discussion about emergency procedures at the center and how to handle mini and major crises.

**Problem solving.** Many of the meetings directors attend or conduct are designed to tackle issues that need to be resolved. The goal of problem-solving meetings is to define the problem, discuss potential solutions, and agree on a course of action. Facilitation techniques such as brainstorming, developing a criteria matrix, and consensus voting are a few of the tools you'll learn about in this book to help you and your team make wise and informed decisions in your problem-solving meetings.

> Naomi held a problem-solving meeting with the teaching staff of her school-age care program. The focus was a child with disruptive and bullying behavior. Naomi helped her staff define the problem, come up with possible solutions, and decide on an action plan for changing the current situation.

**Planning.** Planning meetings are another form of decision-making meetings. The goal in planning meetings is to decide on the sequence and coordination of events or activities—who needs to do what, when, and where. Planning can be short term (assigning tasks and coordinating logistics for an upcoming event) or long term (setting goals and planning strategies for the future). Directors spend a lot of time in planning meetings because the essence of effective administration is the smooth coordination of all the parts of a program. In most early childhood settings, the director is the primary person to orchestrate the parts.

> Naomi's meeting with the center's Parent Advisory Board about the spring fundraising event was a planning meeting. Although Naomi convened the meeting and helped develop the agenda, she turned over the role of facilitating the meeting to the president of the board.

Some of the meetings administrators conduct may be a blend of different meeting types. Others may be representative of a single type. The key is to match the type of meeting with the optimal group size, facilitation style, and room setup to achieve the outcomes desired. The table titled "Different Types of Meetings" summarizes some of these elements.

**DILBERT**

*DILBERT reprinted by permission of United Feature Syndicate, Inc.*

| | Different Types of Meetings | | | |
|---|---|---|---|---|
| | **Informational** | **Professional Development** | **Problem Solving** | **Planning** |
| **Purpose** | Disseminate information | Increase professional competence | Solve problems and make decisions about important issues | Plan, schedule, and coordinate work that needs to be done |
| **Who should attend?** | Those who need to know the information | Those who need to learn the content | Those who have a vested interest or expertise in solving the problem | Those who have knowledge pertinent to the planning process |
| **Number of participants** | Any number | Variable (depends on the topic, desired outcomes, and instructional strategies used) | Optimum 8-15 | 3-10 |
| **Facilitation style** | Typically one-way communication from leader to participants, with opportunities for questions | Combination of one-way and interactive, depending on desired outcomes | Interactive, discussion | Interactive, discussion |
| **Room setup** | Classroom style or U-shape | Classroom style, U-shape, or boardroom, depending on group size and topic | U-shape, circular, semicircular, or hollow square | U-shape, circular, semicircular, or hollow square |
| **Emphasis** | Content | Content and process | Process and outcomes | Process and outcomes |
| **Ensuring success** | Good planning and preparation | Voluntary participation, full engagement | Climate of mutual respect, consensus decision making | Preparation, participation, staying focused |

# Meeting Roles: Who Does What?

Like a Broadway play, a meeting involves a host of roles, each essential to its success. Just who assumes these roles and how they carry them out depends on the type of meeting and the nature of the work to be done. In general, most meetings involve the following cast of characters: convener, facilitator, timekeeper, recorder, and participants.

**Convener.** As director of your center, you are probably the person responsible for convening staff, parent, and board meetings. You may not have thought your role as convener was all that important, but in fact the success of any meeting is largely determined before the participants even arrive. The decisions you make about who to invite, the order of topics to be addressed, the room setup, and how prepared participants should be can make all the difference in how effective you will be in achieving your desired outcomes. In Chapter 3 you'll learn the nuts and bolts of compiling a good agenda and how to plan for success.

**Facilitator.** The term *facilitate* means "to make easy." Thus, the role of facilitator is to make the group's work easy. This means the facilitator must focus on the collective needs and goals of the group and not his or her own needs and goals. The skilled facilitator is adept at choreographing the group dynamics so that what needs to get done at the meeting gets done, and is done in such a way that group members feel invested in the outcomes. Balancing the twin goals of accomplishing meeting tasks and attending to the processes of how the group accomplishes its work is no easy job. It requires skill, tact, patience, and perseverance.

There is no one "right" way to facilitate a meeting. Much depends on your personality, the situation, and the nature of the people in your group. In the ideal world, the meeting facilitator is a person who is neutral and skilled in managing a group of diverse individuals, but not vested in the specific content to be covered. The reality, of course, is that few early childhood organizations have the resources to bring in a neutral third party to facilitate meetings.

As a center administrator, you are probably the one who must both convene and facilitate most of your staff meetings, parent meetings, and board meetings. While you care about the group process, you also care about the outcomes and content of the meeting. If you are to be successful in your facilitator/leader role, however, you must subordinate your personal interest in the outcomes and attend to the greater needs of the group.

In your capacity as facilitator, you are first and foremost a servant of the group, focusing attention on common goals, encouraging full participation, summarizing and synthesizing shared information, seeking consensus, and refraining from using the authority of your role to influence the direction or outcomes of the meeting.

If you are too outspoken, opinionated, or heavy-handed, you will simply never attain participants' full involvement, trust, and openness. This does not mean that you need to give up your own interests. Rather, you must think of your interests as one of many sets of interests to be considered when crafting solutions.

The information in the following chapters will help you develop the skills to become a facilitative leader who creates an open climate, values the participation of all members, and shares your own knowledge and insight relating to content. For certain types of meetings (informational, professional development, and planning) this will be fairly easy. For problem-solving meetings focusing on controversial issues, however, you may want to bring in a neutral third party to facilitate.

Effective facilitators do more than just manage the group processes and ensure that tasks are accomplished. Good facilitators also help the group reflect on and improve the processes they use to achieve the meeting's purposes. In other words, they help others understand their individual and collective responsibility for ensuring the meeting's success. Your long-term goal is to decrease the group's dependence on you their leader.

## The Role of the Facilitator

### The facilitator . . .

- sets the tone and promotes a climate of trust and collaboration.
- puts his or her personal interests and needs after those of the group.
- models respectful behavior, good listening, and open-mindedness.
- helps the group stay focused on one issue at a time.
- encourages full participation, ensuring that all members have an opportunity to contribute.
- protects individuals from being attacked if they express contrary opinions.
- helps the group compare and contrast the viewpoints and ideas that have been offered.
- suggests alternative processes or procedures when the group gets bogged down.
- helps the group resolve issues, solve problems, and find win/win solutions.
- clarifies the thinking of the group by pushing and prodding for mutual understanding during discussion and decision making.
- summarizes and synthesizes what participants have said.
- confirms with participants that their ideas have been accurately captured in the minutes.
- summarizes the progress of the group regularly throughout the meeting.

**Recorder.** Meetings can cover a lot of territory. Lots of information is tossed back and forth—facts, figures, dates, opinions, and promises to follow through. Without a way to capture the key points being discussed, the decisions being made, and the brilliant ideas to pursue at another time, participants have only their own recollections to refer to. We all know that memories are notoriously fuzzy. Recollections of what happened at a meeting often differ, especially when it comes to remembering who volunteered to clean the storage room or repair the broken trike.

One way for the recorder to support the work of the group is to capture key ideas on large sheets of paper for all to see. These posted pages can serve as the group memory, facilitating discussion during the meeting. They can also serve as convenient notes from which minutes can be written after the meeting. Recording the group memory on flip chart pages has several advantages. It helps the group stay focused, mentally and physically. It serves as a convenient and accurate visual record of what transpired at the meeting. And it validates the contributions of those participating.

It is important that the facilitator not serve also as the recorder. The recorder should have neat handwriting, fairly accurate spelling, and the ability to capture a lot of ideas in short words and concise phrases. The person also needs to feel comfortable with the collective editing of the group as ideas are written and posted.

**Timekeeper.** As the term implies, the timekeeper manages the clock ensuring that the facilitator and the participants know when they have exceeded the time allotted for an item on the agenda, when it is time to break, and when it is time to wrap things up. In smaller informal meetings, the facilitator can serve as the timekeeper. In larger gatherings where the agenda is full or the issues are complicated, a separate timekeeper should be designated to remind the group when the time allocated for an item is almost up. The group can decide whether to move toward closure on the topic or change the agenda to allow more time for continued discussion.

**Participants.** An effective meeting depends on participants being fully engaged and committed to productive group processes. That means participants must be on time, come prepared, stay focused, and make relevant contributions when appropriate. Productive participants are aware of their personal impact on the group dynamic. They also recognize the power of nonverbal communication—eye contact, gestures, body movements, seating. First and foremost, good participants are good listeners. They contribute only when they have something meaningful to add to the discussion. They are good at building on the ideas of others to generate new or stronger ideas. In other words, productive participants maintain the forward momentum of the meeting.

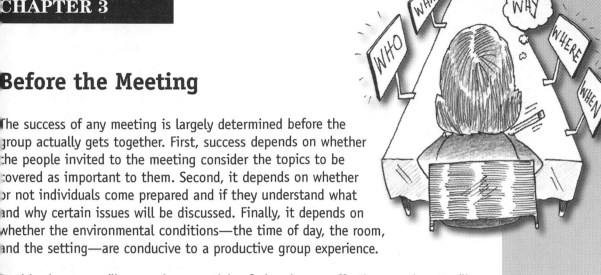

# CHAPTER 3

# Before the Meeting

The success of any meeting is largely determined before the group actually gets together. First, success depends on whether the people invited to the meeting consider the topics to be covered as important to them. Second, it depends on whether or not individuals come prepared and if they understand what and why certain issues will be discussed. Finally, it depends on whether the environmental conditions—the time of day, the room, and the setting—are conducive to a productive group experience.

In this chapter, we'll cover the essentials of planning an effective meeting. You'll learn about the importance of inviting the right participants, developing the agenda, and setting up the environment to ensure a productive and engaging experience for all who attend. Before launching into the specifics of meeting planning, though, we need to stop and ask an important question.

## So Why Are You Even Having a Meeting?

Meeting planning begins with having a clear purpose for hosting a meeting in the first place. This sounds so obvious, but believe it or not, many meetings fail simply because the purpose is not clear in the minds of the convener or the participants. In general terms, you hope of course that individuals come away from a meeting with a better understanding of themselves and others and of the issues that surface during your time together. On a more specific level, however, when you call a meeting, you should have a concrete idea of precisely what you hope to accomplish. Here are a few of the reasons why people come together for meetings.

### Some Reasons Why People Have Meetings

- to analyze
- to build a sense of community
- to celebrate
- to evaluate performance
- to explain
- to find solutions
- to gain support
- to generate new ideas
- to have fun
- to inform
- to identify problems
- to learn
- to make group decisions
- to nurture understanding of others
- to plan
- to promote team cohesiveness
- to reflect on practice
- to solve problems
- to socialize
- to track progress

If you flip back to the chart in Chapter 2 describing different types of meetings, you can see how some purposes are suite to a particular meeting type while others cut across all types of meetings. Undoubtedly, most of the meetings you plan have multiple purposes. In general, though, you should be able to plot the purpose of a meeting on the following continuum, depending on whether people are coming together to hear and learn about new information or whether they are coming together to make decisions and take specific actions.

**Information Oriented**  **Action Oriented**

If the purpose of your proposed meeting falls at the information-oriented end of the continuum, you may want to reconsider whether a meeting is the best format for accomplishing your needs. In other words, should you even have a meeting? There may be a more efficient way to share the information you want people to have than bringing them together face-to-face. When people complain about meetings, one of the most common gripes is that they have to sit and listen to reports, updates, and information on the topic at hand that could be better communicated by being posted on a bulletin board, written in a memo, left as a voicemail message, or sent as an e-mail message.

If we take to heart the feedback about meetings, the first thing to do is decrease the amount of time spent disseminating information. Ask yourself, how imperative is it that everyone have the information? How time-sensitive is the information? Is there a more efficient way to inform people? The underlying assumption in calling any meeting is that people are being brought together to do what groups do best—consider important issues where multiple perspectives are needed.

The purpose of a meeting clearly depends on the history of the group and the organizational context in which it is being held. If the group is meeting for the first time, the purpose and substance of the meeting will certainly be different from those of a group with a long-standing history together. Likewise, if the group will be meeting only one time, the purpose and expectations will differ from those of a group that meets on a regular basis.

The organizational context for the meeting surely has an impact on its effectiveness. If your center is part of a larger agency, for example, it is important to know if your meeting is supported by upper management. If not, a mandate from above may preempt or interfere with full attendance or your group's ability to follow through on the decisions made at the meeting.

Clarifying the purpose of the meeting leads to the next step: clarifying the outcomes you want as the result of the meeting. Visualize what you want to accomplish. Think of your outcomes as a product, not a process. Ask yourself, "How will I know if I have accomplished my purpose for having this meeting?" For example, there is a big difference between "Talk about the traffic congestion at arrival and dismissal" and "Develop a plan to ease the traffic congestion at arrival and dismissal." Being specific forces you to think concretely about the outcomes you expect to achieve by the time people put on their coats and head out the door when the meeting ends.

In general there are two types of outcomes: products (lists, plans, decisions, and agreements made) and knowledge (increased understanding or awareness about an issue). Here are a few examples:

## Products

- Agreement on the key problems with the current billing system for invoicing parents

- An action plan on how to reduce traffic congestion during morning arrival

- Guidelines for using the petty cash fund

- A list of volunteers to work on the spring fundraiser

## Knowledge

- A better understanding of the revised work schedule so that classrooms have adequate coverage at all times

- Increased awareness of how to help children deal with death and illness

Most often when we plan meetings we concentrate on short-term outcomes—those objectives we have for a single meeting. Effective directors, however, know the importance of simultaneously thinking long-term—those broader goals they hope to reach by bringing people together at regular intervals. These goals have to do with building trust, a sense of community, and an awareness of how individual roles and behaviors affect the larger dynamic of the group.

High-functioning groups don't just happen; they are cultivated. One long-term goal for any director who holds regular staff meetings should be helping the group become more effective in managing itself. This means helping the group become highly conscious of how it performs as a collective body. In later sections of this book you'll learn specific strategies to make this happen.

Another long-term goal for early childhood staff meetings is building the overall professional competence of the individuals within the group. Master directors try to infuse into every regularly scheduled staff meeting an opportunity for professional development. This kind of professional development is different from formal in-service workshops on specific topics. Informal, seize-the-moment opportunities help teachers reflect on their roles and broaden their repertoire of knowledge and skills. Professional development can be accomplished through carefully structured warm-up activities, guided discussions around specific topics, or the sharing of best practices by individual group members.

> On the day after the New York World Trade Center disaster, Kathy, the director of a private nonprofit program, distributed to her staff several articles she had pulled off the Internet about how to help children deal with the tragedy. The teachers read the articles in preparation for their staff meeting the following day. They spent the first 30 minutes of the meeting sharing the insights they had gleaned from the articles and talking about how they would respond to different questions the children might pose.

## Who Should Attend?

When individuals complain about meetings, it is not so much that the meeting was poorly run or the content was poorly organized, but that there was a mismatch between the content and the participants selected to attend. All who attend a meeting should have a distinct purpose for being there. If items are going to be discussed or procedures demonstrated that don't really apply to every person, the meeting should be restructured to allow those people not addressed to leave early, arrive late, or not attend at all.

The type of meeting you are hosting determines, in large part, just who should attend. If it is an informational or professional development meeting, you'll want people to attend who need to know or need to learn about the information being presented. If it is a problem-solving or planning meeting, you'll want those attending to have the knowledge and expertise to contribute something valuable to the proceedings. This may also include people who will be most affected by any decisions made.

When deciding who should attend, consider participants' expertise, their interest in the topics to be addressed, and their interpersonal communication skills. This will give you a clearer picture of how the dynamics of the meeting might unfold and whether or not your objectives for the meeting will be met. For example, if your topic relates to a problem you hope to solve, ask yourself the following questions:

- Do the potential participants have the knowledge and expertise to solve the problem?

- Do they have the authority to make the decisions needed to solve the problem?

- What is their level of interest in the issue; do they want to solve the problem?

- What materials or information will they need prior to the meeting to help them develop a mindset for action?

- What is the optimum group size to solve the problem?

When determining who should be included in a meeting, the key factor is relevance. No one wants to spend time in a meeting unless a substantial portion of the meeting is directly relevant to his or her perceived needs. Look carefully at your topics and your participant list. Is there a good match? Should you arrange the agenda so that some participants attend only a portion of a meeting?

If you decide not to invite someone who may think they should be included, be sure to explain the objective of the meeting and why you feel it is not necessary for them to attend. They may agree with you and appreciate your thoughtfulness in not taking up their time. On the other hand, they may disagree with you and provide a rationale for why they should attend. In either case, the person will recognize and appreciate that you have thought about them.

The optimum size for your meeting depends, of course, on the content and purpose of the gathering. For informational meetings, there is really no limit to the size of the group, assuming that questions and discussion can be reasonably handled. Just remember, though, the larger the group, the more formal and less spontaneous the format will be unless you structure the session to include break-out activities in small groups.

The amount of structure you need to impose is directly related to group size. When there are only three to seven people in a group, the flow of business can be more informal and spontaneous and attendees can play multiple roles. The larger the group, the more necessary it is to have clearly defined roles for facilitator, recorder, and timekeeper. For groups larger than 20, you need to impose more structured guidelines for participation. For example, you may require people to raise their hands and limit their comments to a set amount of time.

For problem-solving and planning meetings, determining the optimum number of participants is a bit trickier. The best rule of thumb is to have the smallest number of people possible to achieve your desired outcomes. The size of the group must also be manageable for the tasks anticipated. The ideal number depends on many factors, including the familiarity of participants with one another and the leader's skill in achieving full participation.

The more complex the subject to be discussed in a meeting, the fewer persons should participate.

*Roger Neugebauer*

23

**For problem-solving meetings, invite those who...**

- have knowledge of the topic and can contribute to a solution.
- are committed to solving the problem.
- can afford the time to participate.
- can provide different perspectives on the issue to be discussed.
- feel comfortable expressing their position.
- are open-minded and willing to listen to other perspectives.
- have the authority to make the final decision about what to do.

**For planning meetings, invite those who...**

- have knowledge pertinent to the planning process.
- have the big picture of what needs to be accomplished.
- may be involved in implementing the plan.
- have the time to participate.
- can see how different parts relate to the whole.
- are committed to seeing the plan implemented.

In general, problem-solving meetings are most productive if the group consists of 8-15 participants—large enough to generate a variety of ideas and perspectives, yet small enough to manage the problem-solving task at hand. It is possible to involve more people in problem-solving meetings if the group breaks into subgroups for specific tasks. For example, you might divide the group into smaller groups to brainstorm creative solutions to a particular problem. Subgroups can also generate criteria to evaluate alternatives. These subgroups can then report back to the whole group sharing their ideas. The whole group can then prioritize the proposed solutions and decide on a course of action using one of many consensus-voting strategies. In Chapter 6, we'll explore these strategies in greater detail.

For planning meetings where the task is focused, you'll want to limit the size of your group to a maximum of 10 participants. This is large enough to ensure broad ownership of the plan, yet small enough to ensure that participants can all contribute fully and share relevant information.

## When Should You Meet?

In the world of early care and education, deciding on an appropriate time to hold staff meetings is no easy task. Snatching half an hour or an hour during the middle of the day is very difficult with the tangled web of staff schedules, lunch, and naptime routines to accommodate. Because many teachers have family commitments or second jobs, scheduling meetings at the end of the workday is often not feasible. Despite the obstacles, many administrators have succeeded in staking out a regular weekly or biweekly time to meet with their teaching and support staff. The frequency and time of your staff meetings depend on your center's needs and your working relationship with the staff.

Some directors solve the "when to hold a meeting" dilemma by bringing in teacher-qualified college students or parent volunteers to free-up staff during naptime in the late afternoon when enrollment is lower. Others successfully schedule early morning breakfast meetings before the children arrive. Still others build into their administrative budget overtime compensation so teachers can meet once a month on a Saturday for a longer, more focused interval.

Whatever the meeting schedule you adopt for your center, the key is that your meetings be held regularly, with the dates plotted far in advance so that people can put them on their personal calendars. A "same time, same place" philosophy reduces potential confusion about when and where people should be and helps promote better attendance. Some directors find it helpful to schedule meetings at odd times (1:15 p.m., instead of 1:00 or 1:30) to underscore the importance of beginning on time.

Finding a good time for parent meetings is not easy either. With children to feed, homework to supervise, and dishes to do, parents are often less than enthusiastic about jumping in the car and heading out to attend an evening meeting. Some child care programs solve the problem by scheduling parent meetings at dismissal time and providing food and free child care as an incentive to attend. Others schedule parent meetings on Saturday mornings and provide supervision for the kids on the playground (or in the gym) while the adults meet.

## Developing Your Agenda - Seven Steps to Success

The emphasis you put on developing a formal written agenda and distributing it before your meeting depends on both the type of meeting you are convening and the number of participants attending. If you are convening an informal gathering of four or five colleagues to plan an activity or event, it may be enough to drop them a note or leave a telephone message telling them the purpose of the meeting, when and where it will be held, and any necessary items to bring or think about beforehand. At the beginning of the session, you can develop the agenda together, prioritizing the things you hope to accomplish, the time allotted for specific topics, and agreed-upon outcomes. This agenda generated by the group can be written on the chalkboard or posted on a piece of flip chart paper on the wall.

For more formal meetings with just four or five people where the issue may be serious (or controversial), where the time may be brief, or where the potential for misunderstanding is high, it is wise to have a written agenda detailing purpose, meeting specifics, and anticipated outcomes.

For virtually all other meetings, informal or formal, regular or occasional, where more than six people will be in attendance, you'll want to develop and distribute an agenda beforehand. Time spent in carefully crafting your agenda will be returned a hundred-fold. There is simply no better meeting tool to help you achieve the desired outcomes and promote group satisfaction than a well-formulated agenda that is followed.

An agenda distributed beforehand helps ensure that individuals come to the meeting ready to discuss the issues. It can also set the tone of the meeting. A well-thought-out agenda serves as the group's road map. It provides a sense of direction and gives participants concrete guidelines to structure their discussion.

The best agendas are those developed jointly by the convener and the participants. Careful attention is given to the order of the items to be covered, the length of time each item should be discussed, and who will lead the discussion for each. An agenda should include the date, place, and starting and ending time of the meeting as well as particulars about the items to be considered, so individuals can bring the necessary papers, reports, and data. Here are some suggestions for compiling an effective agenda.

**Step 1: Get input on the topics that should be included.** Soliciting ideas or inviting feedback on items you are considering for the agenda from the participants who will be attending strongly signals that you care about what they think—that the issues and concerns they deem important are also important to you. Inviting input in developing the agenda also lays the groundwork for full involvement. People who have contributed topics to the agenda will be more fully engaged in the meeting since they have a vested interest.

Begin by listing of all items that need to be covered and your best estimate of the time each will take. Break large topics into subtopics. As you consider each topic, make sure it supports the purpose of the meeting. Items tangential to the purpose of the meeting you may want to reserve for another time or deal with in another way (for example, a memo). The key is to keep the meeting focused. As you consider each item, ask yourself if the group is ready to address the issue. Is the timing right for including this item at this meeting? Will the group members be prepared to discuss it or take action if that is your desired outcome?

**Step 2: Determine outcomes and methods for covering each item.** Once you have determined what items need to be covered at your meeting, think about the outcomes you want and the best method for handling each item. If an item is informational, just how knowledgeable or informed do you want people to be after the item is covered? You can think of outcomes for informational items as a continuum from superficial awareness to deep awareness. Being clear about your outcomes in this way makes it easier to decide just how much time to devote to an item, who should communicate the information, and if participants will need a handout or other written pieces to supplement the oral report.

If you are developing an agenda for a problem-solving or planning meeting, think about the outcome you want as a result of the discussion. For example, your desired outcome might be to increase mutual understanding of different perspectives about an issue. It might also be to generate creative alternatives for solving a problem. Being clear about your outcome helps you determine the best method for managing the discussion (for example, round-robin, open floor). If you want the group to reach a decision about an issue, determine what decision-making method will best achieve your goal of getting good buy-in and follow through (majority vote, consensus). The following are some common methods used for different types of meetings. A fuller discussion of these methods will be covered in later chapters.

## Methods for Different Types of Meetings

### Informational

- Reporting
- Questions and answers
- Open-floor discussion
- Round-robin sharing
- Whip-around sharing
- Panel presentation

### Professional Development

- Lecture
- Demonstration
- Panel presentation
- Questions and answers
- Interactive activities
- Assessments
- Pair-and-share exercises
- Large- and small-group discussions

### Problem Solving

- Round-robin discussion
- Open-floor discussion
- Quaker dialogue
- Brainstorming
- Balance-sheet analysis
- Criterion matrix
- Cost-benefit analysis
- Majority voting
- Nominal Group Technique
- Rank ordering
- Consensus decision making

### Planning

- Discussion
- Brainstorming
- Majority voting
- Consensus decision making
- Task and timeline charting

**Step 3. Decide on the appropriate amount of time for each topic.** So many complaints about meetings relate to how time is used. Meetings often go overtime because the agenda is far too ambitious, trying to accomplish too much in too short a time. Giving careful consideration to the amount of time allocated for each item is essential if you want to maintain momentum and allow sufficient time to address each topic included on the agenda. Items requiring discussion and/or decisions will obviously take longer than reports. The size of the group, the seriousness of the topic, and the interactive styles of participants are all important factors to consider when determining the appropriate amount of time to allocate to different topics.

There is no set rule about how long meetings should be, but from the participants' perspective, meetings that are from 1 to 2½ hours in length tend to be viewed as the most productive. Meetings shorter than one hour can be highly productive if the group is committed to starting on time, the agenda is focused, and the facilitator is adept at keeping the group on task. For meetings longer than 2½ hours, breaks need to be scheduled in and careful consideration given to the placement of items on the agenda so that people stay engaged.

**Step 4. Determine the appropriate sequence of items to be covered.** Given the different types of meetings and the wide variety of purposes, there is obviously no "correct" way to structure the order of items on your agenda. Only experience with a particular group can determine how discussion will flow. It is important, though, to structure the agenda so that the meeting starts off on a positive note. This will set the tone for the entire session. That means you'll need to give careful thought to which item should be placed first on the agenda.

As a general principle, try to get involvement from the meeting members within the first ten minutes. This can be accomplished through a warm-up activity, a discussion on a topic that is not controversial, or information sharing. Involving everyone from the beginning creates an expectation of participation that will carry over throughout the meeting.

In determining the order of items on the agenda, strive for balance between items where a single person is dispensing information and items that require the involvement of everyone. The goal is to maintain momentum and sustain interest while encouraging serious consideration of all significant items. Try to avoid two time-consuming items in a row, two highly charged items in a row, or two routine items in a row.

One way to organize the agenda is to divide the allotted meeting time into thirds. Dedicate the first third of the time to general business items that are not controversial. Use the middle third to tackle your highest priority items, handle the most difficult tasks, or address the most contentious issues. The last third of the meeting can be devoted to general discussion items of a less important nature. Try to end the meeting with an item that is upbeat and unifying.

One of the best ways to make the most of meeting time is to dispense with reading of the minutes or committee reports. Send out these summaries with the agenda and ask participants to read committee reports before the meeting. This leaves more time for substantive discussion about items people flagged in their reading of the reports that might need fuller explanation. Encourage people who will be sharing informational items to prepare visuals to augment their presentations. The process of preparing overhead transparencies, flip charts, or other visual aids will help them organize their information and perhaps even simplify or shorten it.

**Step 5. Determine roles.** Making the most of meetings also means making a conscious effort to involve as many people as possible during the meeting. As you develop the agenda, think about how you can share leadership responsibility. Invite others to facilitate the discussion on different topics, serve as recorder or timekeeper, or take charge of setting up the room. The more you involve people in organizing and conducting the meeting, the greater buy-in you'll get. It's as simple as that.

The key is to match the task with the interest and professional competence of the individual you have in mind. Even with seemingly straightforward tasks like preparing the room or acting as recorder during the meeting, you'll want to establish clear guidelines and expectations. Crafting opportunities for staff to participate in meetings is a great way to help them expand their repertoire of professional skills.

**Step 6. Prepare a draft of the agenda.** With a clear sense of the topics you want to cover, the order in which to cover them, and the time allotted to each, you are ready to prepare a draft of the agenda. Note the location for the meeting, the starting and adjournment times, and the agenda items. Where relevant, note the methods to be used in covering specific topic and the intended outcomes. Also, be sure to indicate what items you want participants to bring or what you want them to prepare or think about prior to the meeting. One way to accomplish this is through an annotated agenda: following the topic heading, include a short description and the questions you want people to consider as they prepare for the item.

Give careful attention to the way items are described on the agenda. Use a positive tone and strive for language that is clear and unambiguous. If the group meets regularly, use a template for the boilerplate material—all the information that doesn't change from meeting to meeting. The format you ultimately select for the agenda is a matter of personal choice. The following are several agenda formats you may find helpful as you create your own.

**Group:** Haven Valley School-Age Program
**Date:** September 12
**Time:** 1:00 - 2:30 p.m.
**Location:** District conference room
**Participants:** Janice, Colleen, Margie, Brandon, Martha, A.J., Suzanne, Margo, Jeff, Rachel, Ramon, Donna, Dianna, Cynthia
**Guest:** Sr. Maria McKenna, Principal, St. Mary's School

**Type of Meeting:** Informational, planning

**Facilitator:** Colleen    **Timekeeper:** Ramon    **Recorder:** A.J.
**Refreshments:** Martha    **Room setup:** Janice

**What we need to accomplish:**
We will develop the guidelines for the St. Mary's Parish volunteers who will be assisting with our after-school homework hotline.

**What to bring/prepare:**
Draft of guidelines from summer meeting. One idea for our Columbus Day fieldtrip.

| Topic | Purpose | Time | Person responsible |
|---|---|---|---|
| 1. Personal updates | icebreaker | 10 min. | everyone |
| 2. New timesheet procedures | informational | 15 | Colleen |
| 3. Homework hotline volunteers | finalize guidelines | 45 | Colleen, Sr. Maria McKenna |
| 4. Columbus Day fieldtrip | discussion, decision | 15 | Brandon, Suzanne |
| 5. Wrap up | meeting evaluation | 5 | everyone |

## Logistics

**Date:** October 18

**Start:** 4:00     **End:** 5:45

**Location:** Staff lounge

## Roles

**Group:** JFF Child Development Center staff

**Facilitator:** Joy     **Recorder:** Jim

**Setup:** Jill     **Food:** Annie & Jill

**Type of Meeting:** informational, professional development, planning

| Time | Item | Format | Person | Preparation |
|---|---|---|---|---|
| 4:00 | Warm-up: Halloween share-a-thon | Round-robin | All | Bring one Halloween poem, fingerplay, or activity to share. |
| 4:10 | Update on enrollment and group assignments | Inform | Sandy | Bring the class rosters distributed 9/25. |
| 4:20 | Update on Pumpkin Fest flower sales | Inform | Joy | Bring any new orders that came in this week. |
| 4:30 | Guest speakers for spring parent lecture series | Brainstorming, decision by majority vote | Jeff | Bring your suggestions for speakers, including contact information and samples of books and tapes published. |
| 4:50 | Demonstrate new fire extinguisher and review evacuation procedures for fire drills | Demonstration and discussion | Joy | Read the attached article on safety guidelines for child care centers. |
| 5:15 | Write draft of guidelines and compile sample recipes for parents whose children bring snacks and bag lunches | Discussion, sharing, and decision by consensus | Jill | Bring one recipe for a nutritious lunch or snack that you'd like included in the Healthy Alternatives packet. |
| 5:40 | Meeting summary | Evaluation whip-around | All | |
| 5:45 | Adjourn | | | |

**Raven Street Learning Center—Staff and Advisory Board Annual Retreat
August 18, 2001, 8:00 a.m. – 4:00 p.m.
Raven House Conference Center, Chester Room**

8:00      Coffee, muffins, and time to meet Michelle and Roberto, the newest members of our teaching team
*Think of a completion to the phrase, "You can count on me for..." as you introduce yourself to your new colleagues.*

8:30      Warm-up—Rituals, rituals, rituals *(Everyone)*
*Please read Robert Fulghum's book From Beginnings to End: The Rituals of Our Lives and reflect on the traditions, rituals, and routines in your own life and those that make our center unique. We'll share our reflections during this warm-up activity.*

9:15      Updates and announcements
- Class lists (Janice)
- Bus schedule (Benson)
- Supplies inventory update (Aretha)

10:00      Attracting quality staff *(Marge, everyone)*
*Like the other child care programs in our community, we have experienced a lack of qualified candidates for teaching positions. The situation was particularly acute in our school-age program this past year, where two positions went unfilled for more than a month. Please read the attached article "Attracting and Retaining Quality Staff." Come prepared to share your best thinking about how we can implement recruitment and hiring strategies to attract good candidates.*

11:30      Lunch *(We'll celebrate Jasmine's recent marriage)*

12:30      Improving compensation *(Marge, everyone)*
*Please read pp.107-126 in Taking on Turnover and complete the questionnaires on pp.121-122. Come prepared to share your thoughts about our current job classification system and salary schedule. We'll also brainstorm possible strategies for generating more income for our center and develop a plan for increasing revenue.*

2:00      Calendar planning *(Nadine, everyone)*
*Bring your plan book. We'll schedule dates for fieldtrips, in-service workshops, and rotating responsibilities.  We'll also create a schedule for completing the self-study process for NAEYC reaccreditation.*

3:30      Meeting evaluation

4:00      Adjournment

Your copy of the agenda will be far more detailed than the one you distribute to the meeting attendees. It will include your notes about facilitation techniques you want to use, key points you want to emphasize, and audiovisual equipment you will need at different points during the meeting.

**Step 7: Distribute the agenda.** As a safeguard, it is best to have one or two people review your agenda before sending it out to participants. This helps ensure that there are no glaring omissions in the items to be covered. Also ask these individuals for their feedback on the sequence of items on the agenda and the time allotted to each.

Aim to get the agenda to attendees at least a full week before the meeting. Be sure to attach directions on how to get to the meeting if it is being held at a location unfamiliar to participants and include handouts you want participants to review in preparation for the meeting.

If your center is part of a larger agency or organization, consider sending a copy of the agenda to your immediate supervisor or the agency executive director. This helps keep them informed about the issues you and your staff are dealing with.

## Setting up the Physical Environment

No doubt you've suffered through meetings where a flickering overhead fluorescent light gave you a headache, the room temperature was so unbearably cold you never took off your coat, or the annoying buzz of a lawnmower outside made it impossible to hear what people were saying. How true it is—location, setup, and room comfort can have a profound effect on the success of a meeting.

In setting up the meeting room, try to eliminate potential distractions so participants can give their full attention to the topics being discussed. Assess the overall comfort level of the room in terms of light, heat, and ventilation. Ask someone not involved in the meeting to answer any incoming telephone calls, or hook up an answering machine to record messages. There is nothing quite as disruptive as having the momentum of a good discussion broken by the ring of a telephone.

Since meetings also serve the function of creating a social network, think of ways to encourage participants to feel comfortable with one another and ways to increase rapport. You might want to provide coffee, tea, or soft drinks and perhaps a snack. Be sure to have decanters of water if the meeting is a long one. Individual name tags and name plates (tent cards with the name in bold marker) can help break the ice for a new group. A small vase of flowers and a colorful table cloth can also add a special touch to the occasion.

A good meeting room won't guarantee a good meeting, but a bad meeting room can contribute to a bad meeting.

*M. Doyle and D. Straus*

33

The meeting room should be spacious enough that the group doesn't feel claustrophobic, but not so large that there is a cavernous echo. Give careful thought to the seating arrangement to facilitate good interaction during the meeting. All group members and the facilitator should be able to see and hear each other. Once everyone has arrived, remove unoccupied chairs, moving people as close together as possible. Empty seats are "energy leaks." Get rid of them. A tight, compact group is easier to work with than one that is spread out.

While your options for table and seating arrangements may be largely determined by the furniture available at your center or the hosting organization, make sure your arrangement fits the type of meeting you will be conducting. If you are convening an informational meeting for a large group, a *classroom-style* arrangement may be appropriate. If the meeting includes formal presentations, add a table-top lectern, overhead projector, and screen.

## Classroom Style

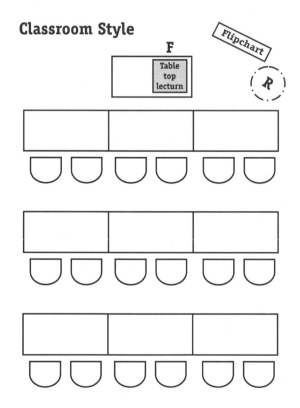

If the purpose of your meeting is problem solving or planning, you'll want to promote feelings of unity and discourage side conversations. *Circular or hollow-square* arrangements are good for these types of meetings because they minimize the status of the facilitator/leader, thus increasing the importance of the participants. Also with these arrangements, there is equal distance between participants, promoting good face-to-face discussion.

P hysical togetherness increases a sense of mental togetherness.

*M. Doyle and D. Straus*

## Circular

## Hollow Square

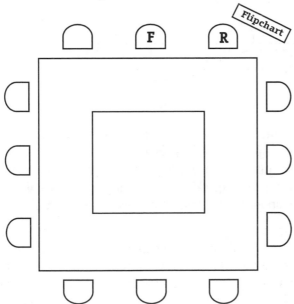

The *boardroom* arrangement, using a rectangular table, creates a greater sense of formality if the facilitator is at the head of the table. If you want to de-emphasize the status of the facilitator/leader, have the individual sit in the middle of the wider side. The disadvantage of this arrangement is that the facilitator cannot make eye contact with all participants. A boardroom arrangement is not particularly good for promoting lively discussion between participants.

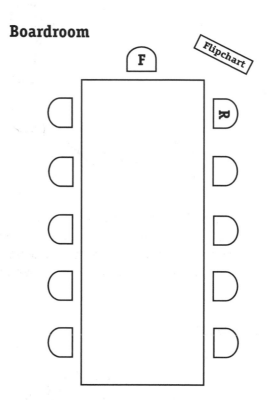

**Boardroom**

A *U-shaped* arrangement is good for an informational or professional development meeting if it involves a presentation or recording participants' ideas on a flip chart. Many facilitators like this arrangement because they can move into the U shape and distribute or collect handouts quickly. While arranging individuals in pairs is easily conducted with this arrangement, small group exercises are a bit more difficult to maneuver.

## U-shape

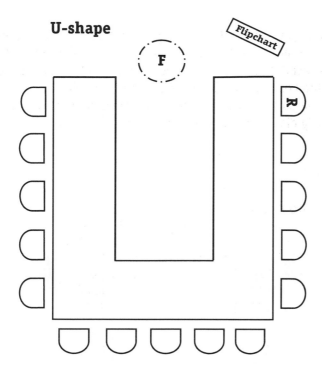

If your group is relatively small and the focus of your time together is problem solving or planning where you will be using brainstorming and charting methods, you might want to try a *semicircular* arrangement. While this arrangement does not provide a writing surface for participants, it does help focus their attention on the task at hand.

## Semicircular

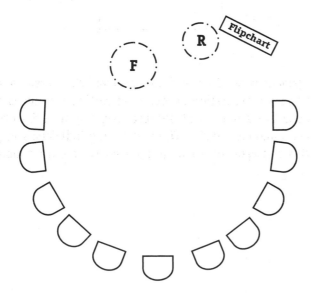

Whatever room arrangement you decide on for the meeting, pay careful attention to where the facilitator and recorder are positioned. The facilitator should have good eye contact with everyone in the group. Likewise, the recorder should be close to the flip chart or chalkboard where notes will be written. If possible, arrange the room so that people coming in and out do not distract the group. Also, position audiovisual equipment so that all participants have a clear, unobstructed view of the screen or monitor.

Finally, plan to arrive early to make sure the room is set up correctly, refreshments are ready, and handouts distributed. If you will be using audiovisual equipment, give yourself extra time to double check that it is operating correctly.

## Meeting Checklist

### Supplies and Equipment

- ❑ flip chart and paper
- ❑ colored felt-tip markers, chalk
- ❑ masking tape
- ❑ tape recorder
- ❑ VCR/monitor
- ❑ overhead projector and screen
- ❑ extension cord
- ❑ laptop computer
- ❑ props (e.g., whistle, bells, posters, hats, talking stick, Koosh ball)

- ❑ welcome sign
- ❑ name tags and name plates
- ❑ extra copies of the agenda
- ❑ minutes from previous meeting
- ❑ list of participants
- ❑ sign-in roster
- ❑ handouts
- ❑ reimbursement forms
- ❑ Post-It Notes
- ❑ refreshments

### Meeting Room

- ❑ window shades
- ❑ tables and chairs
- ❑ room signage

- ❑ location of light switches
- ❑ location of electrical outlets
- ❑ location of heating or cooling controls

### Miscellaneous

- ❑ location of nearest phone
- ❑ location of rest rooms
- ❑ emergency evacuation procedures

✓ **Are you clear in your own mind about what you want to accomplish in your meeting?** Will the meeting serve as a forum for professional development and an opportunity to build staff collegiality, a time to communicate essential information, or a time to solve a problem or plan an event? Knowing your broader goals and purposes for conducting a meeting is the first step in setting the stage for collaboration and shared expectations.

✓ **Does your agenda reflect the input of your staff?** Solicit ideas about potential agenda items from your staff a week or two before the meeting. Find out what issues they would like to discuss. This not only communicates your respect for them as valued partners, but it helps ensure their active participation in the meeting itself.

✓ **Does your agenda reflect only substantive issues that merit the group's getting together?** Meetings often consume enormous chunks of time on topics that could easily be covered in a memo. Don't waste your staff's precious time on trivial matters!

✓ **Have you considered carefully who should attend the meeting?** Your staff does not want to sit through a discussion that has little relevance to their work. Make sure to include only those individuals who will benefit from the information or discussion. If the meeting is to be held when the center is open, make sure you have arranged for adequate supervision of the children and coverage of the telephone.

✓ **Have you set a realistic time frame for discussing the items included on your agenda?** Most meetings suffer from topic overload. Some directors find it helpful to pose a series of questions next to each agenda item to get staff thinking in advance. This can expedite the discussion.

✓ **Did you distribute the agenda several days before the meeting?** To ensure that your staff comes prepared, you will probably also want to send a cover memo and attachments—handouts, articles, or briefing items that they should read prior to the meeting.

✓ **Have you made arrangements for food and room setup?** The environment can be such a powerful influence on people's emotions. Give careful thought to the room arrangement and the small touches that make people feel valued and appreciated. Making the environment conducive to meeting will help focus attention where it should be—on the topics to be discussed.

# CHAPTER 4

# During the Meeting

With your well-crafted agenda in hand and your room set up to facilitate a rich exchange of ideas, you are ready to leap into action. In this chapter you'll learn the nuts and bolts of facilitating a smooth-running meeting, from setting the tone and reviewing objectives to managing the discussion and attending to the group dynamic. Also included are tips for the recorder and minute taker.

## Setting the Tone and Reviewing the Objectives

There are specific things you as the meeting leader can do to establish a welcoming tone that will promote a climate of trust and collaboration. Your body language, the specific things you say and do before the meeting begins, and your welcoming comments set the tone, helping determine whether or not your meeting is productive. Here are some suggestions.

**Pay attention to the mood of people as they arrive.** Make sure you have taken care of all logistical arrangements with respect to room setup, refreshments, handouts, and audiovisual equipment so you can greet meeting members as they arrive. This way you can take time to make a personal connection with each person. This personal connection can give you insight into how the participants feel about attending the meeting—whether they are enthusiastic and looking forward to it or resentful that it is taking them away from other more important things. If you hear grumbling about having to attend the meeting, you'll want to address the issue when the whole group is assembled. "I heard some comments as you were coming in about what a hectic week this is for you. That means our time here today needs to be worthwhile and productive. I will do my part to make sure that happens."

**Start on time.** The way to begin on time is to begin on time regardless of late arrivals. If you wait until everyone has arrived, those who have arrived on time will feel penalized and perhaps be tardy for future meetings. There are many legitimate reasons why people may be late to a meeting, so give them the benefit of the doubt. However, avoid rewarding late arrivers by going over items they have missed. The key is to minimize the distraction caused by their late arrival. Make sure extra seating is close to the door and that handouts are already there for them.

**DILBERT**

*DILBERT reprinted by permission of United Feature Syndicate, Inc*

**Make sure participants know one another.** For meetings where individuals are getting together for the first time or don't know one another well, you'll want to be sure to have name tags and name plates handy and take a few minutes at the beginning for introductions. Taking time for introductions or a welcoming activity helps build group identity and cohesion. It also provides an opportunity to clarify or restate why individuals were invited. Introductions also break the ice, helping people to relax. If participants do not know one another, post on a wall a large diagram of the seating arrangement with everyone's name. It will help people learn each others names.

## Getting to Know You

The time you allocate to introductions varies depending on the length of the meeting, the size of the group, and whether or not the group will be meeting on a regular basis. A quick whip-around sharing of names and affiliations may be sufficient, or you may want to get to know participants in greater depth. Here are some possibilities:

- **What's in a name?** Ask individuals to share the story associated with how they got their name or nickname.

- **Why am I here?** Ask participants to share their expectations for the group and describe their expertise, knowledge, or skill that will contribute to achieving the group's goal.

- **Nerf ball toss.** Toss a Nerf ball to one person and ask that person to disclose something unusual about himself or herself (favorite junk food, favorite childhood toy, hidden talent).

- **Pair and share interview.** Pair attendees with someone they don't know and give them five minutes to interview one another. Each person then introduces his or her partner.

- **What's in my purse or wallet?** Ask members to go through the contents of their purse or wallet and select one item (for example, picture of their grandchildren, key chain from Disney World, lucky charm) that is special or representative of their personality.

- **Spinning yarn.** Give everyone a piece of yarn of differing lengths. Ask them to tell the group about themselves, talking as long as it takes to wrap the yarn around one finger.

- **Stand up and look around.** This is a quick way to acquaint participants with one another in meetings where the group size exceeds 20. Explain that you will be reading a series of questions. If their answer to a question is affirmative, they should stand up, look around, and see who else in the group shares that characteristic. Modify the questions to suit your group, but make sure you have included a sufficient variety of questions so that every person will stand up at least once.

  - Who was born outside the United States?
  - Who has worked in the field of early childhood more than 10 years?
  - Who knows *The Hungry Caterpillar* by memory?
  - Who has been bitten by a child?
  - Who works in an accredited program?
  - Who traveled more than 50 miles to attend this meeting?
  - Who got up before six o'clock this morning?
  - Who likes green tea?
  - Who is left handed?
  - Who has grandchildren?
  - Who thinks our agenda for today is too ambitious?

**Communicate genuine respect for all participants.** Aretha Franklin spelled it out loud and clear in her sensational hit, and the message is still important. People want respect. Meetings are more productive if they are conducted in a climate of trust and respect. While trust needs to be earned and may take some time to build, respect is something you can provide immediately. Respect is communicating through words and actions that each participant's presence is valued. It is conveyed by showing courtesy and consideration, presuming positive intentions, and being an attentive listener.

**Review the agenda and meeting goals.** A smooth-running meeting starts with a shared vision of what you want to happen in your time together. Because you have compiled the agenda, you obviously have a clear sense of what you want accomplished by the end of the meeting. You now need to convey that to the attendees and elicit their collective buy-in to the agenda and the purpose of the meeting. This can be done by briefly reviewing the items on the agenda and restating the anticipated outcomes. "Are we in agreement about the outcomes we want from covering these agenda items? Is the order of items appropriate? Is the time allocated to each topic adequate?"

This part of your meeting will probably take no more than five to ten minutes, but it is crucial for establishing an understanding of what you are going to do and how you are going to do it. In many cases you will need to make modifications to your agenda, reordering some items or adjusting the time.

**Review meeting roles.** Review the different roles people will play during the meeting, including who will act as recorder for the group memory, who will take minutes, and who will lead the discussion on different issues.

**Establish ground rules.** If meetings are to be effective, all members must see themselves as sharing responsibility for creating a climate that is conducive to getting the work done. Developing a set of ground rules—a code of conduct—for how meetings should be run is one way to build understanding about desired meeting processes. A code of conduct is really a working agreement describing how people want to relate to each other. It needs to be drafted, discussed, and agreed upon by all. Most important, it should be reviewed regularly.

If the meeting is a one-time event, you can establish the ground rules prior to the meeting with any co-planners, present them to the group, and ask for their approval. If the group meets regularly, however, use a more participatory approach to developing ground rules. Examples of ground rules are provided in Chapter 5, along with a suggested sequence for developing them with your staff or any other group that will be meeting on a regular basis.

**Conduct a warm-up activity.** Try to plan an inclusion activity within the first ten minutes of your meeting. This helps develop a comfort level among participants and focus the group's attention and energy. The warm-up activity can serve as a springboard for introducing the major topic on the agenda. It should be strategically planned so it supports the group's needs and purposes. For a meeting where the topic may be contentious or where individuals have questions and reservations, the warm-up activity can be structured to bring out those questions or concerns.

If you are leading a regularly scheduled staff meeting that covers a variety of topics, the warm-up activity may be structured to build collegiality and understanding among participants. One way is to do a quick "checking in" activity, having each person provide an update and any concerns or distractions they have brought to the meeting. For example, "I had a bad reaction to the flu shot I got yesterday, so I'm feeling kind of wiped out today." "My husband's company is downsizing, and we are uncertain what the future holds for us."

If the purpose of the meeting is to generate ideas to solve a problem or come up with new ways of working, then you'll want to conduct a warm-up activity that gets the creative juices flowing and helps people think "outside the box." For example, you can create dyads and distribute a familiar item to each pair (for example, pencil, penny, stick of gum, ruler, sponge, or paper clip). Ask each twosome to come up with as many creative uses they can think of for the item. Another creativity booster is to ask people to come up with a book title to describe their life or a movie title that captures a typical day on the job. You'll find other ideas for warm-up activities in Chapter 6.

**Project a tone of energy and enthusiasm.** The words you use and your voice intonations can strongly influence how lively and spirited your meeting will be. Remember, conducting a successful meeting is a lot like running a successful circle time with a group of four-year-olds. Adults, like preschoolers, can be challenging when it comes to getting and holding their attention. Sustaining interest requires maintaining the momentum. Good meetings have a rhythm—things keep moving, but not so fast as to leave people in the dust. Momentum is also achieved by voice intonation. Think of the pitch and volume of your voice as an important facilitation tool that you can use to signal changes in the flow and importance of discussion topics, create energy, and communicate respect to all participants.

## Balancing Task and Process

Leaders of high-performing work groups are able to maintain a balance between task and process during meetings. Task refers to the WHAT of a meeting. This includes such things as setting goals, making decisions, solving problems, and the content on the agenda to be covered—creating a budget, planning an event, or developing a marketing plan, for example. Process refers to HOW the meeting is conducted. It includes the ways in which individuals are involved in dialogue and discussion, how decisions are made, the overall climate and tone of the meeting, opportunities for expressing creativity, and the emphasis placed on making interpersonal connections.

When a meeting is too task oriented, discussions may be closed off prematurely and the needs of individuals who must implement the decisions may be overlooked. If a meeting is too process oriented, issues may not get resolved, momentum may wane, and individuals may loose sight of the task to be accomplished.

| Task Oriented | Process Oriented |
|---|---|
| Setting goals and objectives | Connecting and socializing with colleagues |
| Disseminating information | Hearing all perspectives |
| Making decisions | Attending to personal needs |
| Attending to details | Brainstorming |
| Following the agenda | Nurturing interpersonal understanding |
| Solving problems | Encouraging full discussion |
| Planning work | Attending to people's feelings |
| Watching the clock | Paraphrasing for validation |
| Learning new skills | Valuing creative thinking |
| Staying on task | Probing for understanding |
| Scheduling events | Respecting diverse opinions |
| Coming to closure | Providing recognition |

Managing both task and process is the essence of effective meeting facilitation. It is not easily achieved because the people who attend your meetings are far from homogeneous in their dispositions. Some will be more task oriented and want you too move through the agenda at top speed. Others will be more process oriented and expect you to take a lot of time deliberating on every issue.

Since a group is a collection of individuals, each with a set of personal needs, values, beliefs, personalities, and problem-solving styles, how you manage the group dynamic as it relates to task and process determines your ability to achieve the meeting goals. Depending on the composition of the group, you may be perceived as too rigid and controlling or too wishy-washy and indecisive. Clearly, striking the right balance between task and process is not easy.

# Working Your Way Through the Agenda

In the previous chapter we talked about the importance of a well-crafted agenda as a roadmap for your meeting. But even a well-crafted agenda can't guarantee that you won't encounter a few potholes along the way. After all, meetings are about people, and people are seldom predictable. Your role as the facilitator is crucial for keeping the group on track. As you make your way through the agenda, here are some general pointers to keep in mind.

**Introduce each agenda item.** Provide participants with some background information on the topic, the method that will be used to deal with the issue, the desired outcomes, and the time allocated. Invite clarification about how the item will be treated before proceeding. Sometimes just reminding the group about the boundaries and parameters of a particular issue can prevent the group from getting sidetracked.

**Cover only one agenda item at a time.** This principle sounds like common sense, but it is violated regularly in meetings. Dealing with only one issue at a time is important because the nature of group interaction will pull the meeting in multiple directions. For example, a discussion about an issue like lunchtime transition schedules invariably raises questions and concerns about other issues, like the content of the children's menus, licensing standards, or the brand of catsup the center buys. It is easy to get diverted or jump ahead. Your role as facilitator is to ensure that the group finishes one item before going on to the next and avoids considering tangential items.

To keep the group focused, you may find it helpful to post on the wall a sheet of flip chart paper labeled The Parking Lot or Odds and Ends. On this page you can note items or topics that come up during discussion that you want to address at a later point. This reassures participants that you haven't forgotten their concerns and that you'll get to them at another time.

**Set a comfortable pace.** Try to match your pace to the group's needs. The momentum can be established by starting the meeting with a few quick items. This gives the group the sense that they are making progress and are productive. Difficult or contentious items should be interspersed with quick, easy items to keep the meeting from getting bogged down. A responsive facilitator recognizes when the discussion has gone beyond the point of being useful, when people are beginning to repeat themselves, or when interest is beginning to wane. You don't want to leave people behind in the dust, but you also can't persist on issues so long that momentum is lost.

**Ensure broad participation.** Broad participation doesn't necessarily mean that everyone has equal air time, only that everyone has an opportunity to express his or her view on an issue. Individuals certainly differ in their interest, ability, and comfort level in expressing themselves orally in group situations. Using a variety of methods to elicit input during a meeting helps ensure that even quiet members of the group have an opportunity to air their opinions and ideas. During the meeting, tune in to participants' body language and nonverbal cues to sense if feelings and behavior are congruent. If people appear to be holding back on an issue, you may want to take steps to encourage a more open expression of ideas. In Chapter 6, you'll find some useful strategies to broaden participation.

**Encourage good listening.** Respectful listening is a skill that can be learned. As facilitator, your role in both modeling good listening and reinforcing good listening as a norm of the group dynamic in essential. Participants sometimes are so preoccupied with what they themselves are going to say that they don't bother to listen carefully to what others are saying. Encourage participants to restate the position of the previous speaker before stating their own thoughts on an issue: "John, before you provide a response, would you summarize Ann's position for us?"

**Don't be afraid of silence.** People need time to think and respond. Silence can signal that people are processing what has been said. Be patient with the quiet. Appropriately used, silence can help create a comfortable environment for thinking. It communicates respect for the depth of thought and reflection you expect from the group.

**Tune in to nonverbal clues.** Nonverbal communication—facial expressions, posture, the way we move and sit—can convey powerful messages that are often more telling than words. Effective facilitators are keenly aware of nonverbal communication and can spot indications of participants' frustration, boredom, or withdrawal. Be alert as well to the seating patterns of groups that meet on a regular basis. It may be necessary to occasionally stir up the seating arrangements to break up cliques or reduce the incidence of sidebar conversations.

**Monitor the group's energy level.** When people seem to be losing interest in a topic, showing signs of frustration, or just stuck on an issue, you may need to intervene. You can do this in one of two ways. You can try to re-energize the group with your own energy: open the window, move around the room, pump up your level of enthusiasm, and show a heightened interest in the issue at hand. Or make the group aware of its own sluggishness and have them and decide what to do. "It appears we've hit a wall on this issue. Would you like to take a short break or table this topic for the time being?"

I t's a mistake to think we listen only with our ears. It's much more important to listen with the mind, the eyes, the body, and the heart.

*Mark Herndon*

**Provide closure for each agenda item.** Make it clear to the meeting participants when you have completed one item and are moving on to the next. This can be done by giving a short summary of the discussion that has just taken place. If discussion of an agenda topic has resulted in a decision, state the decision in full sentences, checking that all participants interpret it in the same way. This also aids the recorder in taking more accurate minutes. "I've heard three reasons during our discussion about why we had such low attendance at the parent orientation. Before we move on to making a recommendation for next semester, let me recap these reasons: 1) the invitation got mixed in with the children's other papers, so some parents didn't receive it; 2) the date conflicted with the elementary school curriculum night; and 3) parents of returning students didn't know we would be covering new information."

**Keep one eye on the clock.** If you've assigned a timekeeper for your meeting, you can rely on that person to signal you and the other members of the group when the time allocated for a specific agenda item is nearly up. If you are serving as timekeeper and facilitator both, place your watch on the table in front of you and check it periodically while you manage the discussion. Serving as both facilitator and timekeeper is challenging. It takes sensitive assertiveness to break the momentum of a discussion and help the group redirect its focus. If it is clear that the topic needs more deliberation, ask the group if they want to extend the time limit for the item by adjusting the remainder of the agenda or table the item for completion at a later date. Be mindful that even these negotiations eat up time. Managing the clock is not easy, but it is essential if your group is to stay on task and accomplish what it has set out to do.

## Managing the Discussion

Your job as facilitator includes tracking how a group is progressing in any particular discussion. This is easier said than done. Seldom does a discussion move in a linear fashion from presentation of an issue to its resolution. It is often a messy, convoluted process. Unrelated issues get tossed into the mix, people get sidetracked, emotions flare. People use terms that are vague or open to multiple interpretations, thus causing confusion about what has been said or left unsaid.

Every discussion, however, should have a beginning where you state the methods that will be used to hear from everyone (for example round-robin sharing of ideas), a middle where you help refocus the group if some aspects of the issue haven't been addressed, and an ending where you summarize the key points made. Here are a few suggestions for managing the discussion in your meetings.

- **Paraphrase.** Paraphrasing serves two purposes. It communicates that you have listened carefully to what people said, and it provides a concise summary to the other participants of what has been said. Paraphrasing should not be *parrot-phrasing*. It involves restating in your own words what you have heard, not just repeating it verbatim. When you paraphrase someone's words, you are essentially asking them, "This is what I think you said; am I correct?" Here are some other ways you can paraphrase: "Jillian, let me make sure I understand you. You believe that the current weekly payment system for parents is confusing and should be revised." "Lana, so you are saying that the new pick-up policy will create a hardship for parents who also have children at the elementary school?"

- **Probe for clarification.** If you think an individual's point may be misinterpreted by others, check for understanding by probing for greater clarification. "Patricia, are you suggesting that we should speak to parents individually rather than sending out a survey to get their feedback?"

- **Expand.** Use the comments made by individuals to get the participants in the group to broaden their consideration of the issue. "You've provided insight into how the assistant teachers will view the new rotating responsibilities. Let's also consider how the lead teachers will interpret the change."

- **Relate comments to previous contributions.** Making connections between the contributions of individual members of the group promotes team building and collaboration. "Crystal, your statement of how Tiffany got so upset when her mother left this morning is a great example of what Gayle was talking about earlier in her presentation on attachment theory."

- **Ask individuals to elaborate on ideas.** Asking for examples and illustrations helps the group move the discussion from general, broad constructs to greater specificity. This aids in mutual understanding. "LaToya, that's an interesting point you've made about the outdoor schedule. Can you give us some specific examples of how it has impacted your afternoon routine with the two-year-olds?"

- **Refocus the discussion when needed.** When joking, personal stories, or irrelevant side talk goes on too long, refocus the discussion on the agenda topic. "Your personal stories of dealing with the accounting department at central office have certainly added some levity to our meeting, but we need to get back to our discussion about the purchase requisition procedures. We have ten minutes left to come up with a recommendation for change."

- **Check the group's understanding.** Many, if not most, of the words we use in everyday conversation have multiple meanings. In fact, the 500 most commonly used words in the English language have more than 14,000 dictionary definitions. When an individual in the group uses an acronym, jargon, or specialized terminology that may not be familiar to everyone, intervene to check for understanding. "Does everyone understand what Michelle means when she refers to the accreditation self-study process?"

- **Encourage specificity.** Ask individuals to be more specific if they use words or phrases that are too general, vague, or open to multiple interpretations. "Carmelita, you've said that the parents are upset with the new policy. Do you mean *all* the parents, or just *some* parents who are very vocal about how this policy has adversely impacted them? Out of 22 parents, how many have actually voiced concerns?"

- **Question hyperbole, hearsay, or unsubstantiated statements.** Facilitators play an important role in helping participants temper exaggeration and discern facts from personal opinions. Intervene with tact and sensitivity as needed. "Barb, do you know for certain that the bus service is going to change its schedule, or could it be just a rumor?"

- **Try to find areas of agreement in conflicting points of view.** When conflict occurs in groups, skilled facilitators deemphasize areas of disagreement and focus instead on areas of shared understanding or interest. "Wendy, you and Marina appear to have very different opinions about the role of the senior volunteers in the after-school program, but I am hearing that you are both committed to using the volunteers. Is that true?"

- **Share your feelings.** Sometime the best way to help keep a group focused and moving forward is to be open in sharing your feelings about how the meeting is progressing. Making your thoughts transparent can help build a collective appreciation for the difficult role you play in balancing task and process. "I feel somewhat frustrated. We've gotten off the topic of our role in the agency visioning retreat. I sense that the group is more interested in venting feelings about the recent personnel changes at the central office than it is in planning our part in the retreat."

During the discussion, try to crystallize statements into phrases that can be recorded as part of the group memory on flip chart paper or in the meeting minutes. Later in this book you'll learn specific questions you can use to broaden discussion, rein it in, redirect, or refocus it. When a discussion centers on task-related problems or issues (for example, coming up with a new emergency evacuation plan, determining rotating responsibilities, scheduling parent volunteers), your role in managing the discussion is usually pretty straightforward. When the focus of the discussion is on people-related issues (values, perceptions, expectations, needs, concerns), however, your role is far more difficult. These instances call for tact and sensitivity, and often skill in conflict resolution. In Chapter 5 you'll learn strategies for dealing with these more difficult situations.

Remember, in your role as facilitator your goal is to serve the group by guiding the processes of the meeting and promoting the expression and understanding of others' ideas. The meeting should not be a platform for promoting your own opinions. If you have information to share, opinions to offer, and a point of view you are eager to express, be careful that you don't use your authority as meeting leader to manipulate the outcome of a discussion or decision.

The danger of simultaneously serving in dual roles, facilitator and group member, is that you may unconsciously or consciously choose a process, structure a discussion, or filter the information shared that it leads to the outcome you want. If you do this, the group will feel betrayed and you will lose credibility the next time you facilitate a meeting with this group. Participants may also stop contributing if they feel their ideas are not valued or have little impact.

If you are conducting a meeting and individuals consistently defer to you during group discussions and decision making, it may be a clue that you have exercised your authority in ways so that prevent people from taking risks, speaking freely and frankly, or offering contrary points of view. Monitor how much you are talking. Do you talk after each contribution to the group? Is the flow of conversation always directed through you, or are connections made directly between individual members of the group? Try to let the meeting participants do at least 80% of the talking.

When individuals do defer to you, boomerang questions back to the group, expressing your opinion or ideas on an issue only after everyone else has had an opportunity to speak. If group members have an entrenched pattern of nonparticipation or lack of risk-taking, it may take some time to reverse this norm and communicate your serious intent on broadening participation.

Becoming an effective facilitator does not happen overnight. It requires patience and practice and sensitivity to the group's nonverbal signals. With practice you'll learn to readily sense when members feel discouraged, frustrated, confused, or just plain bored, and redirect the discussion to keep up the pace. Effective meeting facilitators are flexible, adapting to the needs of the group and altering the agenda if necessary to keep involvement and interest high.

# Capturing the Group Memory

A good recorder with the right tools and skills can make meetings more effective by creating a *group memory*. The two most common techniques for recording are charting ideas on large sheets of paper during the meeting and writing up and distributing minutes after a meeting.

Charting ideas on flip chart paper during a meeting creates a visual record of the group's progress that can simulate discussion, improve participation, and document decision making. Writing up and distributing minutes after a meeting serves to remind people about who said what and how a particular issue was decided. Minutes also serve to keep individuals who missed the meeting informed about what transpired.

If you have developed an agenda for your meeting, you are aware of the topics where it would help to have a recorder available to capture key points made, ideas generated, or decisions arrived at by the group. It is important to determine who will serve as the recorder before the meeting so the individual can come prepared mentally for the job and bring the necessary tools—notepad or laptop computer, flip chart paper, markers, and tape.

For most meetings it is sufficient to have one person serve as recorder. For some meetings, however, you may want two people filling the role—one person to take detailed notes that will later serve as minutes for the meeting, and another to chart the group's ideas on large paper to facilitate discussion, planning, or decision making during the meeting.

**Charting ideas on large pieces of paper.** Charting ideas on large pieces of paper during a meeting has several advantages. Charting frees participants from having to take notes, encourages greater participation because group members see that their ideas are important enough to be recorded, helps latecomers see what they have missed, and reduces repetition in discussion. Charting creates a sense of accomplishment because participants can see the work they have done. It also gives them the opportunity to make sure their comments are interpreted accurately.

Visual learners in particular appreciate this technique in meetings. When they can see an idea in print, they have an easier time understanding and remembering it. Flip chart pages can be labeled and stored for future reference, or they can be used in preparing minutes summarizing accomplishments of the meeting.

The recorder should have reasonably neat handwriting, good spelling, and the ability to capture a lot of ideas in concise phrases or sentences. Charting is an art. The key is to write down the gist of what people say in their own words. Abbreviations are acceptable as long as everyone can understand what they mean. The recorder may need to ask participants to summarize long ideas. The person can also be responsible for managing the Parking Lot or Odds and Ends—the group's ideas and issues to be discussed at a later time.

Recorders need to be aware of the power that comes with the role so that they don't abuse it. The ideas committed to paper and posted during a meeting can surely influence the direction of a discussion, so accuracy is important. The group needs to feel comfortable correcting the recorder if errors have been made or the visual notes don't accurately reflect what has transpired during the meeting.

The recorder needs to make it clear to the group when he or she is contributing his or her thoughts, ideas, and opinions to the visual record. He or she should also feel comfortable enough to ask if ideas have been captured accurately. Your group may want to consider rotating this role so participants all learn the skills needed to effectively capture the group's memory.

## Tips for the Recorder

- Post flip chart paper so it is visible to everyone in the room.

- Write or print clearly, with letters large enough for everyone to read.

- Use water-based, color felt-tip markers—dark colors (blue, black, green, purple, or brown) for the text and bright or light colors (orange, yellow, red, or pink) for headings, underlining, bullets, borders, and boxes.

- Alternate colors for different items to make them more readable. Use bullets, borders, and boxes to make items more identifiable and underlining or capital letters for emphasis.

- Use pictographs, symbols, or graphics as appropriate to capture the relationship between ideas or activities.

- Summarize key points made during the discussion using the same words and phrases of the speaker. Check for clarification as needed.

- Use acronyms and abbreviations only if everyone in the group understands what they stand for.

- Leave room in the margins so you can add extra notes or ideas as the meeting progresses.

- Use a separate sheet of paper labeled Parking Lot or Odds and Ends to post issues or topics that need to be handled at a later meeting.

- Number pages consecutively and post in sequence on the wall.

**Writing and distributing minutes.** Most directors of early childhood programs do not have the time or the secretarial support to type up elaborate minutes. Even so, it is important to provide a written summary of the highlights of the meetings you conduct. The information helps inform those who could not attend, refreshes the memories of those who did attend, and serves as a valuable record of the group's progress.

The minutes should include the date and time of the meeting, names of those who attended, and topics discussed. Capture the key points covered in the meeting, including important decisions made, actions taken, agreements to follow up, and issues needing further attention. Minutes can be posted or they can be duplicated and distributed to individuals who attended or those who could not attend. Be sure to save a copy, along with your meeting agenda and handouts you distributed, for your archives.

Effective minutes are brief, accurate, well organized, and distributed soon after the meeting. Minutes can help achieve buy-in of those who attended by letting them see that their ideas and words are now part of the permanent record of the group. Many directors also send copies of their minutes to others they want to keep informed about different program issues (board of directors, agency executives, community leaders). Think of your minutes' potential as a public relations medium.

Like the agenda, the format for the minutes depends on the formality of the group's proceedings and how the minutes will be used. Even if you rotate the role of recorder at your meetings, try to follow a consistent format for summarizing the minutes. This will create a trademark for your group, minimizing confusion for those who regularly read the minutes. You can choose a style that is essentially narrative—capturing ideas in full sentences—or a more abbreviated form relying on bullets and short phrases. Appendix A is an easy-to-use format that many directors have adopted. The advantage of using this Action Minutes template is that it can be completed during the meeting and distributed promptly afterward.

## Wrapping Things Up

No doubt you've attended meetings that simply ran out of time—where people were gathering up their belongings, putting on their coats, and preparing to make a mad dash for the door while the facilitator was frantically trying to wrap up unfinished business. If the experience left you frustrated, you are not alone. One of the most frequent complaints early childhood practitioners make about meetings is that they don't end on time. They also report that there is a lack of follow through on the decisions made at meetings. These two complaints are obviously related. If the leader is too rushed to summarize what has transpired at the meeting, people are more likely to leave without a clear sense of who is responsible for carrying out what decisions.

Devoting a slice of the meeting agenda to wrap-up activities is crucial. Psychologically, this gives a sense of closure to your work. A formal wrap-up helps you and the group tie up any loose ends, decide what to do about any unresolved issues, and celebrate the accomplishments of the day. All these steps are important to maintain commitment and ensure follow through.

Plan to wrap up your meeting at least ten minutes before its scheduled adjournment. This allows enough time to summarize actions taken, review agreements to follow up, and debrief on the success of the meeting. There are several things you'll want to accomplish in this portion of the meeting.

**Review the "leftovers."** It is possible during your meeting that there were agenda topics that needed further discussion or items posted in the Parking Lot that need to be put on the next agenda.

**Review all decisions and action plans.** This review helps everyone understand the decisions that were made about what will be done, by whom, and when. Identify clearly what is expected—a report, a plan, the convening of a task force or subcommittee. Be specific when asking for volunteers or delegating assignments. *Anybody can do it* often turns out to be *nobody does it*.

If a discussion on a specific topic ended with only a verbal commitment by participants to follow through, you may want to use some time during your wrap-up to solidify commitments. Ask individuals to write down on a piece of paper three steps they will take to follow up and ensure that the decision is carried out as discussed. Have them share these written commitments for action publicly with the group.

**Draft your agenda for the next meeting.** You'll already have a jump on developing the agenda for the next meeting from reviewing leftovers that didn't get completed at this meeting. Elicit other suggestions and decide on the time and place for the next meeting.

**Celebrate the group's accomplishments.** Taking time to acknowledge the accomplishments of the group reinforces a shared commitment to goals. If the group has tackled a particularly thorny problem or accomplished an important task at the meeting, take a few minutes to do a quick wrap-up activity that focuses on the group's achievements. For example, ask everyone to think of a newspaper headline that captures the accomplishments of the day ("Cherry Creek Child Care Center Rolls Out Balanced Budget"; "Toddler Teachers Tackle Child Assessment Plan").

There is nothing worse than continuing a meeting with people slowly wandering out. It's like sitting in a bathtub and watching the warm water drain out around you.

*M. Doyle and D. Straus*

**Celebrate individual learning.** If the meeting included a professional development component, you'll definitely want to give people a few minutes to reflect on what they learned. This can be done in a variety of ways. You can simply do a round-robin sharing where everyone highlights one new idea or concept that they can apply in their work, or you can do a more elaborate creative activity that helps people synthesize new learning. For example, distribute felt-tip color markers and strips of paper about three inches wide and two feet long. Ask people to create a bumper sticker that captures one new insight they gleaned during the meeting, a quote they don't want to forget, or a pearl of wisdom they value.

**Thank everyone for their contributions and participation.** Recognition for work is so important for sustaining commitment. Give a verbal pat on the back by acknowledging the contributions of various people to different topics on the agenda and of the individuals who assisted with room setup, food, and other meeting logistics. You can also make this a round-robin activity, allowing individuals in the group to acknowledge one another for specific contributions. "Shelly, I really appreciated your candid feedback about the bulletin board displays." "Mark, thank you for your honest comments about what it is like to be a male working in child care."

**Evaluate the meeting.** Take a few minutes at the end of each meeting you facilitate to allow participants to assess the effectiveness of the meeting. Meeting evaluation serves two purposes. It gives you concrete feedback that will help you become a better facilitator, and it gets people thinking about their own role as a meeting participant. With groups up to 15, evaluation can be done informally as a whip-around exercise, providing 30 seconds per person to comment on any aspect of the meeting or the group dynamic. You can leave this open ended, allowing individuals to comment on any aspect of the meeting, or you can ask them to complete a sentence stem. Here are some possibilities:

- I am leaving this meeting today feeling...
- I am happy that we...
- I came expecting... I am leaving...
- I am concerned that we...
- One thing I enjoyed about today's meeting was...
- At our next meeting, I hope we can...
- One thing that might improve our future meetings is...

If you are running short on time, or if you don't want to put people on the spot, you can use the following option on page 58.

Any group too busy to reflect about its work is too busy to improve.

*Robert Garmston*

Select three questions from the following list of questions. Write each question on the top of a separate sheet of flip chart paper. Tape these sheets of paper near the exit of the room. During the meeting wrap-up, distribute three small Post-It Notes to each participant. Ask them to answer the three questions using the following scale: 1 = *not at all*; 2 = *somewhat*; 3 = *completely*.

As individuals exit, they can post their ratings to the three questions on the appropriate sheets of paper. From this feedback you'll have an instant assessment of your meeting effectiveness in three areas. For future meetings you can select different questions or come up with completely new ones that you and your group develop.

- Did the meeting achieve its objectives?

- Did the facilitator stick to the agenda?

- Did the meeting meet your personal needs?

- Was your time well spent attending this meeting?

- Did you feel personally invested in this meeting?

- Was participation balanced during the meeting?

- Did the facilitator keep the group focused on its task?

- Do you think the meeting was productive?

- Was communication open and direct?

- Do you feel your input during the meeting was valued?

If you want to do a more structured assessment of the meeting, consider using Appendix B "Meeting Evaluation" or Appendix C "Checklist of Effective Staff Meetings." No matter which method is used, your evaluation should be focused on methods for improving the meeting, not judging or blaming individuals. The feedback generated from these assessments will help you determine what changes need to be made in the structure and process of future meetings to make them more effective.

For groups with which you meet regularly, such as your own staff, it is wise to devote a full meeting once a year to the topic of meetings. Taking time to reflect on the structure, content, and processes of your meetings helps your staff become more invested in future meetings.

# CHAPTER 5

# The Group Dynamic

Good meetings do more than just cover content; they also
serve as forums for helping people understand group dynamics
and each person's role in contributing to the group process.
Just as individuals have unique personalities, so too does the
collective group. In some groups it is clear how member's diverse
styles mesh to create a healthy tension that supports the group in
achieving its goals. Like the individual gears on a ten-speed bicycle
that must work in sync for the bike to operate smoothly, in high-functioning
groups the collective body achieves a kind of synergy that allows it to achieve far
more than any one individual could do alone.

If you have ever been part of a high-functioning group, you have experienced the
palpable energy that results when individuals serve different but complementary
functions that create a vibrant group dynamic. You have also no doubt been part of
a group where self-serving behaviors prevailed, where the tension between and
among participants sapped the vitality of the group, preventing it from achieving
its goals. Such dysfunctional groups are akin to the gears grinding on the bicycle.
When people posture for attention, promote self-serving agendas, or emotionally
and mentally withdraw, the group is temporarily or permanently prevented from
achieving its goals.

In this chapter you'll learn how facilitators can create a shared responsibility for
meeting success among group members. You'll learn about the importance of
working agreements, the roles people play in groups, how rituals and traditions can
unite people, and how different communication and personality styles can either
create negative tension or support positive group functioning.

## Participants' Responsibility for Meeting Success

Productive groups pay equal attention to accomplishing the work of the group and
building harmonious relationships among members. This is a responsibility that
must be shared by all members of the group. An important part of your role as
facilitator is to help meeting participants become conscious of how their actions
support or inhibit the work of the group. There are many things you can do to
promote this awareness.

**C**ooperation is spelled with two letters – WE

**Use inclusive language.** If your goal is to promote norms of collaboration in your meeting, the three most important words you can use are *we, us*, and *our*. These are words of inclusion, cooperation, and alliance—the essence of collaboration. Think consciously about how you structure your comments so that you define common interests, concerns, and benefits. To the degree that you are able to move from *I* and *you* to *we, us*, and *our* in both your words and your actions, you will begin building the norms of collaboration needed for collective responsibility. If you are convening a meeting with a group for the first time and want to stress how important it is that everyone contributes to the group process, you might want to distribute "Nxxdxd Vxry Much!" as a handout and talk about what it means for your group.

## Nxxdxd Vxry Much!

Xvxn though my typxwritxr is an old modxl, it works quitx wxll xxcxpt for onx kxy. Thxrx arx 46 kxys that function wxll xnough, but just onx not working makxs thx diffxrxncx.

Somxtimxs it sxxms that our group is somxwhat likx my typxwritxr: not all thx kxys arx functioning propxrly. You may say: "Wxll, I am only onx pxrson. It won't makx much diffxrxncx." But, you sxx, for thx group to bx xffxctivx, it nxxds thx activx participation of xvxry pxrson.

So thx nxxt timx you think you arx only onx pxrson and that your xffort is not nxxdxd, rxmxmbxr my old typxwritxr and say to yoursxlf, "I am a kxy pxrson and am nxxdxd vxry much."

**Make evident the group's shared values.** Meetings can be powerful ways to both establish and reinforce shared values. Values are what we stand for, those guiding principles or ultimate truths that are important in our lives. It stands to reason that people who share common values will have greater potential to work effectively together. During the meeting, help participants to articulate their individual values and identify those they share with others. This is important because shared values become the foundation for a shared vision in early childhood programs. "Chanice, it sounds like you and Tanya feel strongly that we should try to accommodate the cultural traditions that the parents practice at home. How does the rest of the group feel about this issue?"

**Reinforce interdependence.** A sense of interdependence occurs in meetings when individuals see how their input contributes to something greater than what they could achieve by themselves. You can promote feelings of interdependence during the meeting by providing focused feedback that links individuals' efforts to the larger goal of the group. "Connie, by building on Mark's suggestion and coming up with a new idea about organizing the curriculum library, you showed how much more we can achieve when we work together."

**Encourage people to be direct with one another.** If your goal is to create norms of open, direct communication in the group's interactions, it is important to praise those who take risks to "put it out there," raising important issues that might be uncomfortable for the group to hear or deal with. When candid conversations occur, let the group know that you value their commitment to being forthright and direct with one another.

**Acknowledge those who are not present.** How powerful it is for a facilitator to occasionally remind the group of an individual who is not present at the meeting. "What would Janice think about this issue? What would she say if she were here today?" You might even want to make a paper cut-out of the person and put it in one of the seats if you know the individual will be absent from the meeting and you want to make sure that his or her presence is felt and respected.

**Provide specific feedback to participants.** If you meet with a group on a regular basis, you have a vested interest in providing feedback to individuals about their behavior at the meetings you lead. Feedback can be informal and periodic, but it should be specific and focused. Don't pass up an opportunity to provide positive feedback when someone that was helpful in keeping the discussion on track, relieving tension, providing energy and inspiration, or giving emotional support to another person. "Courtney, I really appreciated the leadership you took during our meeting yesterday when you suggested that we all stand up and give Rachel a round of applause for organizing the Pumpkin Fest. I know that meant a lot to her coming from one of her colleagues."

**Promote respectful dialogue.** The media bombards us with examples of adversarial interactions. Television commentators and radio talk show hosts regularly frame discussions using pros and cons, point-counterpoint, good versus bad, and other polarities to make points and defend positions. These examples carry over into the conversations people have at work. It is no wonder that in many meetings, discussion is often reduced to verbal combat between participants. The loudest and most persistent voices are heard. Modeling and promoting respectful dialogue can lead to a more productive meeting environment.

Respectful dialogue requires skills that can be learned and practiced. It is characterized by suspending judgment, being open to conflicting data, and not considering someone with a different point of view as an adversary. When individuals engage in respectful dialogue they are willing to expose their reasoning and underlying assumptions. They also signal their interest in exploring differing viewpoints more broadly and deeply.

The language of collaboration is all about creating relationships

*Jack Griffin*

61

## Behaviors that Support Group Productivity

Although most of us don't consciously think about it, any time we are involved in a group, our actions and behaviors affect the group process. Some behaviors support getting the job done:

- initiating ideas
- seeking information
- providing information
- clarifying and elaborating
- summarizing
- evaluating
- testing for closure

Other actions and behaviors focus on group relations and help members feel comfortable and connected. These behaviors help build team cohesiveness, interdependence, and commitment to group goals:

- encouraging
- harmonizing
- gatekeeping

Both types of behaviors are essential if a group is to be productive. If you are meeting with a group over an extended period of time, or if you regularly facilitate meetings for your own staff, help individuals become conscious of these different behaviors.

To raise their awareness of their behavior in meetings, consider having them complete "Contributing to Meeting Productivity: What Role Do I Play?" found in Appendix D. You might want to distribute this assessment tool prior to an annual retreat or other gathering where you will be focusing on the topic of meetings. You can use the results as the springboard for a discussion about how your group can work together to improve meeting effectiveness.

## Establishing Ground Rules

For groups that meet regularly, it is wise to develop a working agreement—a set of ground rules or meeting norms—to serve as a code of conduct. Developing ground rules for how meetings should be run is one way to build understanding about desired meeting processes. Ground rules describe how people want to relate to each other. They need to be drafted, discussed, and agreed upon by all. Most important, they should be reviewed often, preferably at the beginning of each meeting. You might even want to laminate your meeting ground rules and post them in your staff room.

Meeting ground rules should cover the mechanics of your meeting (for example, when and where the group will meet), meeting procedures (how decisions will be made), and desired behaviors (common courtesies you want displayed). Your ground rules should not be viewed as a set of regulations that will hamper the group's creativity. Rather, they are a set of flexible indicators to support the group in working productively together. Because every group is unique, the same set of ground rules will not be appropriate for all groups.

If possible, ground rules should be established in the early stages of the group. If new members are added to the group, you'll want to reestablish consensus about the rules. To initiate the process, ask members to reflect privately on the characteristics of a good meeting. Then ask them to record their ideas on separate slips of paper or index cards. In a round-robin sharing, invite members to share their items with the whole group. Consolidate items that are similar and reword them as needed to come up with a final set of guidelines that everyone can support. Decide on what your group would like to call its completed document—working agreement, meeting guidelines, code of conduct, or simply meeting rules. As you work with your group to develop a set of ground rules, consider these categories:

- **Attendance.** Does everyone have to be present to hold the meeting? How many people must be present to conduct business?

- **Time.** When will the group meet? How is "on time" defined? How will you help latecomers catch up? What are people's responsibilities when they know they'll be late? How will the group minimize the distractions that can occur with late arrivals?

- **Participation.** How will discussion be managed? How will full participation be encouraged?

- **Confidentiality.** Are there topics that should not be discussed during the meeting? Is there information that should not be shared outside the meeting?

- **Interruptions.** How will participants who "have the floor" be respected? Can participants be called out of meetings? How will phone calls, pagers, and other interruptions be handled?

- **Preparation.** What are expectations regarding preparation for the meeting? What if people cannot complete their assignments?

- **Meeting roles.** Who will serve as convener, facilitator, recorder, and timekeeper? Will roles rotate?

- **Flexibility.** How will a balance of process and task be ensured?

- **Decision making.** How will different types of decisions be made; majority vote, consensus?

- **Evaluation.** What method will be used to evaluate your meetings; how often, and by whom?

- **Violation of ground rules.** How will the group respond if the ground rules are not followed?

## Happy Valley Preschool Code of Conduct

**We will strive to...**

◆ be punctual, respect time limits for agenda items, and stay for the entire meeting.

◆ come prepared.

◆ communicate openly and directly.

◆ be courteous, listen attentively, and be respectful of different points of view.

◆ participate fully and not engage in sideline conversations or distracting behaviors.

◆ be flexible and open to change.

◆ stay on task and not divert attention to unrelated topics.

◆ assume that others' intentions are positive.

◆ focus on opportunities and possibilities, not dwell on roadblocks and excuses.

◆ strive for consensus in decision making; if an impasse is reached, a simple majority vote will be used.

◆ make decisions based on what is best for children and families, not what is expedient or easy.

## Rituals and Traditions

The rituals and traditions you establish as part of your meeting culture help make the group distinctly different from any other. Rituals and traditions help connect us to our past and provide a bridge to the future. They create community, a sense of belonging, and a unique group identity that can turn common experiences into uncommon enriching events. Most important, rituals and traditions provide a way to convey shared values, underscoring the things group members cherish most.

If you regularly facilitate meetings for your staff or another group, think of some things that you can do to infuse deeper meaning into your gathering, reinforce the importance of connections, and make the experience more memorable. The most powerful rituals are reflective—they affirm the importance of what we do in the service of children and families. They also provide a sense of consistency and shared expectation that help anchor the group. Think deliberately about rituals and traditions you can begin to establish to

- launch a new school year

- welcome newcomers to your team

- celebrate accomplishments

- honor exemplary service

- provide a sense of closure to a project

- celebrate birthdays, holidays, seasons, or special events

Rituals and traditions need not be grandiose, but they also shouldn't feel contrived. What is important is that they provide an opportunity for participants to reflect, connect, and in some small way experience life's deeper meaning.

- One director holds her annual staff retreat at a campground located about an hour from her center. The teachers all bring tents and sleeping bags and hold a late-night powwow around the campfire while they munch on smores and sip hot chocolate.

- At the monthly staff meeting at another center, teachers take turns reading a children's book out loud and leading a discussion about how the book might be incorporated into a circle time discussion.

- To reinforce the importance of working toward a common vision, a director of a Head Start program has the center's mission statement made into a large poster. He then cuts the poster into puzzle pieces, giving each teacher a piece. At the first staff meeting of the new school year, teachers decorate their individual pieces and talk about how their personal goals support the center's mission. After they assemble the puzzle, they pose with it for their official group photograph.

## Accommodating Different Styles

When people with differing sensory styles, communication styles, and decision-making styles work together, the potential for chaotic interactions is high. This means that dealing with misunderstandings is part of the facilitation game. Meetings provide a wonderful opportunity for directors to help staff appreciate the diverse ways of taking in and processing information. The goal is to increase people's tolerance for those who see the world differently.

Without ceremony to honor traditions, mark the passage of time, graft reality and dreams into old roots, or reinforce our cherished values and beliefs, our very existence could become empty, sterile, and devoid of meaning.

*T. Deal and K. Peterson*

E very person is like *every* person is some ways. Every person is like *some* other person in some ways. Every person is like *no* other person in some ways.

*C. Kluckhohn and H. Murrary*

Copyright© 1987, Eureka Woods Publications. Reprinted with permission.

While there are numerous ways to describe personality differences, three that clearly impact meeting effectiveness are sensory style, communication style, and decision-making style.

**Sensory style.** We use our senses to make connections between what we know and what we don't know, and to express that understanding. Over time, each of us has developed certain preferences or perceptual modalities. Individuals with a strong *visual* modality appreciate meetings where there is a printed agenda, handouts, and visual aids such as overhead transparencies. Those with an *auditory* preference tend to be good at recalling the information discussed. They enjoy discussions and appreciate good speakers. Finally, individuals with a strong *kinesthetic* perceptual modality appreciate meetings that include interactive exercises, role-playing, and activities where they can get up and move around.

**Communication style**. How we engage in conversation during meetings has a lot to do with our individual communication style. Some people like to express themselves verbally; they process information while they are speaking. Others are more reflective, speaking only after they have carefully thought through what they want to say.

- *Spirited* communicators tend to be animated and lively in their speech patterns and gestures. You can count on them to inject enthusiasm into your meeting.

- *Direct* communicators are candid and decisive in their speech patterns. They take a no-nonsense approach, seldom holding back. You can count on them to "tell it like it is," but they may also be viewed as too forceful by some of their colleagues.

- *Considerate* communicators are good listeners, easygoing, and patient. They are great team players, but may get frustrated when colleagues with a spirited or direct communication style dominate the discussion.

- *Analytical* communicators like to present information in a logical, orderly manner. They tend to be focused, detailed, and precise in the way they express themselves. They can be counted to analyze all the details of an issue, but may be perceived by some as being too rigid or inflexible in their thinking.

**Decision-making style.** Some people have a strong need for closure and are *quick* decision makers. They review the facts, make a decision quickly, and then want to move on. Other people have a more *deliberate* decision-making style. They are more cautious in their approach, preferring to keep options open and explore all facets of an issue thoroughly before making a decision. Clashes between quick and deliberate decision-making styles surface early and resurface often in meetings. As the facilitator, you need to be aware of your own decision-making style preference and make sure you use a balanced approach when dealing with individuals with a different style.

## Dealing with Difficult People

You are bound to encounter difficult participants sooner or later in your role as facilitator. It's inevitable. To be sure, all of us can be difficult at times, but there are some people who make a habit of being difficult. Because self-serving behaviors can have a negative effect on a group and sabotage the group's efforts to achieve its goals, it is important to recognize unproductive behaviors and deal with difficult people before their behavior becomes an established pattern in the group.

Self-serving behaviors are those that meet an individual's needs at the expense of the group. Sometimes difficult people are conscious of their behavior; other times their behavior may be the result of a personality blind spot. Here are some self-serving behaviors you have probably witnessed in the meetings you have attended or facilitated.

- The **monopolizer** hogs the air in the room, dominating the group discussion. This individual offers an opinion on anything and everything, even when his or her opinion has not been asked.

- The **agitator** disagrees openly, provokes arguments, and expresses opinions in a confrontational tone.

- The **pessimist** can be counted on to offer the worst-case scenario when suggestions are tendered by other group members. This person sees only obstacles, not opportunities, and is often persuasive in describing why new ideas won't work.

- The **joker** introduces inappropriate humor or sarcasm during a meeting, attracting attention and detracting from the work of the group.

- The **whisperer** carries on disruptive and annoying sidebar conversation while the meeting is going on.

- The **rambler** strays from the agenda, introducing irrelevant issues that take up time and divert the group from the work at hand.

- The *know-it-all* likes to posture for attention, trying to impress the group with his or her knowledge and expertise. This person usually expresses little interest in what others offer.

- The *lobbyist* has tunnel vision, focusing only on a single issue or pleading a single cause. This person sounds like a broken record playing the same song again and again.

- The *withdrawer* is physically present, but has emotionally and mentally checked out of the meeting.

- The *quibbler* takes delight in splitting hairs, focusing on inconsequential details of items being discussed.

- The *gossiper* delights in offering tidbits of hearsay about people's personal lives.

- The *headshaker* provides disapproval through nonverbal actions such as raising eyebrows or crossing arms or through an exasperated guttural sound or click of the tongue.

- The *interrupter* consistently starts talking before other people are finished.

- The *straggler* habitually arrives late for meetings (or from breaks).

Dealing with difficult people presents a real challenge to the facilitator. Your goal is to reduce the incidence of the self-serving and disruptive behavior but not alienate the difficult person. When dealing with problem people, begin with the least threatening intervention. Isolated instances can simply be ignored or you can acknowledge the person's action by describing without evaluating.

For example, when the headshaker rolls her eyes or makes a disapproving groan to something that has been said, you might say, "Sylvia, it looks like you don't think sending out another parent survey will make any difference. Am I correct?"

When the monopolizer is dominating the discussion, you can say, "Jason, I appreciate your thoughts on this issue. However, it might be good to hear from some of the others. Would those of you who have not spoken care to add your ideas to those already expressed?"

When the quibbler threatens to derail the conversation by focusing on minutia, you can intervene gently, "Thanks for calling our attention to the details of this proposal, Jose. Let's address the big picture first, and then we'll return to examine some of the finer points you've raised."

You can also try to turn the negative behavior into positive behavior. For example, a monopolizer can be assigned the role of recorder and asked to summarize people's comments at the end of a discussion. The joker might be asked to lead a light-hearted warm-up at the beginning of the meeting to reduce the need to be the center of attention during the meeting. The straggler can be assigned a role early on the agenda or right after breaks and reminded of the importance of his or her contribution to the team effort.

If the self-serving behavior persists and has a negative impact on the group dynamic over a period of time, then you'll want to talk with the person in private. In your discussion, presume positive intentions and try to ascertain if the person knows the behavior is unproductive.

Sometime people do things that have a negative impact on a situation that they did not intend. It could be that a monopolizer, for example, feels he or she is contributing great ideas to the group and doesn't perceive the behavior as dominating the discussion. It could be an interrupter is just overly enthusiastic, has lots of ideas, and isn't aware that he or she is cutting people off. It could be the withdrawer has personal concerns that are preventing full participation in the meeting.

Describe the situation to the person without excess emotion. Pick your words carefully so they are descriptive, not evaluative. For example, instead of saying "Why are you always so pessimistic?" tell the person the effect that the behavior has on you as group leader and on the other participants. "When you came up with your list of reasons why Shawna's proposal wouldn't work before she had even finished presenting all the details, it put a damper on the discussion and prevented us from coming up with other creative options."

Sometimes, just helping the person become aware of the negative consequences of his or her behavior is enough to trigger a personal commitment to do better. Other times it may be necessary to make a plan for reducing or eliminating the disruptive behavior. Even if you are not able to eliminate the self-serving behavior altogether, you may at least be able to reduce its negative effect on the group.

## When Conflict Occurs

The facilitator wants to make sure that the meeting is safe, but safe doesn't necessarily mean comfortable. In fact, if a group's meetings are always comfortable, it probably means that the group isn't tackling substantive issues that relate to people's values and beliefs. Addressing these issues may introduce conflict, but it is the kind of conflict that can lead to better decisions, greater group cohesiveness, and a deeper commitment to shared goals. Effective groups regard conflict as an opportunity to improve interpersonal understanding rather than something to be avoided.

Think of conflict as a continuum with minor disagreements and misunderstandings at one end and serious differences and confrontation at the other end. When two or more people begin to focus on each other's personalities rather than their ideas, and when petty bickering threatens to derail the work of the group, it is incumbent upon you to intervene and redirect the group's energy more constructively. If you feel the group is becoming immobilized by the tension, there are several things you can do.

**Acknowledge the tension.** If emotions are high and conflict seems imminent, acknowledge the tension that exists in the group. This in itself can help diffuse some of the emotionality around the issue. "I sense that this is a hot topic for several of you. I wonder if we might take a minute to go around the table and share a single word that captures how you are feeling at this moment."

**Emphasize that diversity of opinions is important and needs to be encouraged and supported in the group.** Reminding the group that conflict is the natural outcome of deeply held views reaffirms people's right to hold strong beliefs and exhibit passion about those beliefs. Passion about one's beliefs, however, doesn't preclude people from interacting respectfully, seeking mutual understanding of differences, and working to see if there is common ground. Help the group separate differences of opinion from personal attacks on the individual holding the opinion.

**Help clarify the source of the conflict.** Conflict occurs when people have different facts about an incident, different values or beliefs about something, different perceptions about an issue based on their own previous experiences, or different needs and priorities. Conflict in many centers occurs from a lack of clarity about roles—who is supposed to do what, how, and when. Conflict can also result from simple misunderstandings about the meaning of words.

As facilitator, you can help individuals discern the difference between *fact* (something that actually exists), *inference* (a logical conclusion based on fact), *speculation* (a theory based on conjecture rather than fact), and *opinion* (a strong belief about something). The most difficult conflicts to resolve are those resulting from differing beliefs and values. If individuals use words like "should" or "ought to," the conflict or dispute is probably related to a difference of deeply held values.

**Insist on respectful listening.** When people are emotional about an issue, it is easy to forget basic courtesies of respectful listening. Intervene if necessary: "Carmen, I can tell you feel strongly about this issue and are eager to share your point of view, but I wonder if you could let Rhonda finish describing what happened before you jump in."

T o disagree, one does not have to be disagreeable.

Conflict can often be defused if people are given the opportunity to articulate their viewpoint without being interrupted. You as facilitator need to be the judge of when people have had an opportunity to state their case without allowing them to rehash it over and over. It is important to check for understanding and summarize after a person states his or her case. "Olivia, I don't believe that was what Jess was saying. Before you describe your objection, would you tell us what you heard him say."

**Look for common ground.** Rather than focusing on the different positions, look for common ground or mutually held interests from which to work out a resolution. "Sara, it looks like you and Jill have different priorities about how to spend the proceeds from the spring fundraiser, but you both agree that a committee of teachers and parents should make the final decision."

**Take a break.** If the emotional climate of the meeting has gotten too heated, or if people seem to have reached an impasse, it may be necessary to table an issue until additional facts can be gathered and people's emotions have subsided. If you decide to take a break or table an issue, be sure to reassure the group (and particularly those individuals most vested in the issue) that you are not minimizing the importance of the issue by postponing its resolution until a later time.

**Reinforce conflict resolution.** When the group has successfully dealt with conflict, be sure to reinforce and acknowledge their ability to meld differences into workable solutions. This signals an important norm for the group—that conflict is not something to be avoided, but rather something the group has the capacity to handle in respectful, constructive ways.

**90%** of friction is caused by the wrong tone of voice.

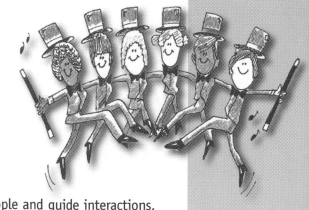

# CHAPTER 6

# Strategies for Enhancing Meeting Effectiveness

When participative approaches are used to involve people and guide interactions, meetings can become powerful vehicles for energizing and motivating people to higher levels of performance and commitment. In this chapter we'll explore some additional tools of the trade for effective meeting facilitation. You'll learn strategies for getting people involved, asking the right questions, solving problems, and making decisions. These facilitation skills and interactive processes will help you enhance participation and ensure greater involvement in the meetings you lead.

## Getting People Involved

People participate in groups when they have something to say and they feel it is safe to say it. Participation can be broadened by thinking strategically before and during your meeting about how to maximize involvement. Here are a few suggestions.

**Create an agenda that promotes involvement.** It stands to reason that the more that people have an active say in the topics included on the agenda, the more invested they will be during the meeting. As you plan the agenda, think about specific ways to involve people. Rotate responsibilities such as setting up the room, preparing refreshments, serving as recorder or timekeeper, and conducting the warm-up activity. The more that leadership is shared, the greater stake people will have in ensuring meeting success.

**Conduct a warm-up activity that includes everyone.** Conducting a warm-up activity at the beginning of your meeting is a great way to get people energized and involved. Warm-up activities should be short and crisp. A warm-up that takes little preparation is to simply have each person answer, in 30 seconds or less, a question distributed before the meeting. The question can serve as a springboard for introducing the main topic of the meeting, or simply relate to an issue relevant to all those attending. Here are some possibilities:

- What is one incident you handled with a child this week that made you feel proud?

- What is one activity or instructional strategy you observed another teacher doing this week that you would like to try out?

- What is your pet peeve about the way space is organized in the center?

- What was the nicest thing a parent said to you last week?

- If an anonymous donor gave a million dollars to the center, how would you recommend we spend it?

**Draw on the energy of the extroverts, but don't forget the introverts.** Clearly some people are more extroverted and enjoy the spotlight in meetings. Capitalize on this personality disposition by asking them to lead discussions, share their expertise, or play devil's advocate. While the extroverts are an asset for generating energy and keeping the momentum going during meetings, don't overlook the introverts who tend to be more introspective in their style. Introverts also have opinions and need a meeting climate that values their contributions.

To keep outspoken extroverts from overshadowing the introverts, use a round-robin method for sharing ideas on an issue. Simply go around the group asking people if they have a response or comment to make regarding the issue being discussed. Allow people to pass if they have nothing to add, but monitor time carefully if they do speak so that everyone gets equal time on their soapbox.

**Cultivate a learning community.** Try to include in each staff meeting a short professional development segment of at least ten to twenty minutes during which teachers share a new resource, field trip idea, classroom management tip, or curriculum activity. As an alternative, have each teacher read a chapter from a book and summarize it to the group. If the staff have recently attended a professional conference, they can use the same reporting strategy to share what they learned. Your goal is to create the norms of a learning community where all members contribute to the sharing of best practices.

**Guide the discussion to include all participants.** You know you've conducted a good meeting if everyone leaves the meeting feeling that they've had an opportunity to be heard, and that when they spoke, other folks really listened. Unfortunately, this is not the case in many meetings. During some meetings, competition for air space is so fierce, that if people stop to catch their breath while speaking, they've lost the floor. Achieving the right balance during meetings so that no one person dominates the discussion and all feel free to express their viewpoint is no easy task.

If you have a group that is particularly outspoken or has a few members who interrupt a lot, you may find it necessary to develop guidelines for taking turns. Raising hands is obviously the easiest option, but in some meetings even requiring people to raise their hands doesn't control the chaos. The interrupters just start talking as they put their hand in the air, not even waiting to be called on to speak. If this is what happens in your meetings, try using an object to signal a person's turn to speak. You can use a talking stick, a toy microphone, or toss an object such as a beanbag or Koosh ball to the individual who has the floor. That person then tosses the object to the next person who has been called on to speak. A person may not speak unless he or she is holding the object.

Another technique to add some decorum to turn taking is a variation of the Quaker dialogue. This is a discussion method that promotes equal participation and respectful listening. Go around the table inviting each person to speak to an issue for a designated period of time without being interrupted. People are free to pass if they want to, but no one is allowed to comment on any other contribution until everyone has had a chance to speak. Before opening the floor to general discussion regarding the ideas raised, ask those who passed during the first round if they have anything to say.

**Have fun.** Adding a bit of levity to your meetings can reduce the likelihood of the snooze factor settling in. Spontaneous or programmed fun energizes people and increases involvement.

- In preparation for a strategic planning meeting, one director sent each member of the board a copy of *Who Moved My Cheese?* For the dinner before the meeting, she served cheese fondue.

- At another center, the director surprised her teachers by having students from the local massage therapy institute give foot massages during a staff meeting. The gales of laughter captured the staff's delight with this surprise.

- The director of another program invited a caricature artist to attend one of her monthly staff meetings. The woman sat in the back of the room sketching cartoon caricatures during the meeting. When the meeting ended, everyone left with a personalized gift in hand.

## The Art of Asking Questions

The right questions strategically asked at the right time during a meeting can create the synergy needed to unlock the potential of the group. Asking good questions comes with practice. Effective facilitators have honed their technique over time. As they try out different kinds of questions with different groups, they keep a mental scorecard of those that are most effective. The skillful use of questions can stimulate discussion, promote greater interpersonal understanding, and strengthen collegiality among members.

Questions can be loosely grouped into two categories. Those that are direct and are intended to elicit specific factual information: "How many parents attended the orientation meeting?" And those that are open ended and are intended to stimulate discussion and promote deeper reflection about issues: "What are some of your concerns about the new schedule?" If overused, direct questions can make people feel like they are being interrogated. Use them only when necessary. Open-ended questions elicit far greater involvement from people.

In general, open-ended questions posed to the whole group are less threatening than those directed to a specific individual. Some people just don't feel comfortable being put on the spot. Try also to avoid asking leading questions such as "Don't you think...?" or "Wouldn't you rather...?" Leading questions reveal your bias—something you'll want to avoid if your goal is to stimulate multiple perspectives and points of view.

L aughter is the shortest distance between two people.

E ffective leaders motivate people not by the answers they give, but rather by the questions they ask.

## Questions to promote participation

- "What do you think about the proposal as stated?"
- "Would anyone care to offer additional insights to help us better understand this issue?"
- "We've heard from several people. Before we move to making a decision, would those who have not spoken like to add anything to the discussion?"
- "Leatha, what is your reaction to Jamie's suggestion?"
- "Carmen, what has been your experience in dealing with this problem?"

## Questions to move people to a deeper level of analysis

- "What are some other ways we might address this issue?"
- "The suggestion you gave was appropriate for our part-day program. Would it also be appropriate for our full-day program?"
- "Bonita, what do you mean by difficult transitions?"
- "Beth, would you give us an example of what you mean by out-of-control behavior?"
- "John, would you expand on that idea for us?"
- "What is the worst-case scenario if we make the change as proposed?"
- "What other aspects of this problem should we explore?"
- "What is the difference between what is happening now and what you'd like to see happen?"

## Questions to help people achieve consensus

- "Many good ideas have been presented. Will someone please summarize what we've agreed on so far before we move on to the next issue?"
- "It appears we have come to an agreement on this issue. Does everyone feel comfortable with the plan as Becky summarized it?"
- "I sense from the heads I see nodding that many of you like the idea Jessie proposed. Are we ready to see if we have sufficient agreement to move forward with this plan?"
- "It appears we are almost ready to make a decision. Are there any loose ends we should consider before we take a vote?"

**Questions that reflect what people are thinking or feeling**

- "Sheila, I sense that you are not satisfied with Pat's answer. Is that right?"
- "Chad, your comment suggests that you don't feel comfortable moving to the next issue so quickly. Is that true?"
- "Kendra, your body language tells me you are uncomfortable with the way Toni has characterized the situation. Is that right?"
- "Chelsea, you seem hesitant to express your thoughts on this issue. Is there something that was said that has upset you?"
- "I sense that this is a difficult issue for many of you around this table. Should we adjust the rest of our agenda so we can deal with this issue now rather than waiting until our next meeting?"

# Planning Tools

No doubt many of the meetings you lead will be planning meetings to work out the details of who, what, where, when, and how a certain project, event, or activity will unfold. Planning meetings are typically more task focused than other kinds of meetings. The goal is usually clear—to develop a detailed list and scheduling of the tasks, timelines, people responsible, and resources needed to carry out and complete the project, event, or activity.

By their nature, planning meetings are future oriented. The facilitator must tap participants' linear and sequential thinking skills to help them envision how to get from point A to point B. When done right, planning meetings also generate a "**T**ogether **E**veryone **A**chieves **M**ore" spirit as people see the synergistic effect of pooling their talents and energy into a coordinated effort.

Here are the steps you'll want to follow to orchestrate the development of a plan. How much time you spend on each step will vary, of course, depending on the size of the project, event, or activity; the number of people involved; and the group's previous experience in working with one another.

**Step 1. Think about the end product.** Your end product could be a report or handbook, a social event, an in-service workshop, a ceremony, a new playground, or even a new curriculum for your center. Some plans will be grand; others more modest. Allowing people the opportunity to think out loud about the end product is important because it gives them a chance to talk about their vision for what they want to occur. For example, if it is an event your group is planning, the elements of that event include not only the activities people will be doing, how they will interact, or what they learn at the event, but also how attendees will feel about the event.

In asking your planning group to talk about their visions for their ideal event, encourage them to reflect on the specific descriptive words they have chosen. *Professional, fun, exciting*, and *inspiring* are just a few of the words people could use to describe an event. Talk about how the words your group has used can become indicators for measuring the success of the event later on.

**Step 2. Generate a list of all tasks that need to be done.** You can have people write tasks on Post-It Notes or index cards. The key is to put only one task on each card. Questions will immediately surface among the group about the degree of specificity needed. Obviously this varies with each plan. At this stage in the planning process, tell people not to worry about the order of the tasks, just to write as many as they can think of. For small projects you may have only ten to twenty tasks; for large-scale events, you could easily have 100 or more tasks that need to be done.

**Step 3. Estimate the time needed for each task.** As you generate realistic estimates of the time needed to accomplish each task, you may end up consolidating some tasks or dividing others. Cluster the individual tasks into natural groupings depending on the type of plan you are developing. For example, if it is a professional conference your group is planning, you could have clusters of tasks for space, food, speakers, registration, program, exhibitors, evaluation, and public relations.

**Step 4. Assign responsibility for each task.** If your planning group is small, assigning responsibilities may be done at a single session when everyone is present. If the group is planning tasks for others who will carry out the work, it may be necessary to consult those individuals first before completing this step. In either case, *everyone* should be aware of every task that has been assigned and who is responsible for it. Certainly some tasks may involve more than one person.

**Step 5. Organize tasks chronologically and assign deadlines.** If you are planning a project such as writing a handbook or conducting a research study, the tasks you come up with may fall naturally into some logical, sequential order. In planning a major project or a large-scale event, however, many tasks will need to be carried out simultaneously. For each task, you need to ask, "What has to be accomplished before this task can begin?" "What tasks can't begin before this one has been completed?"

The most realistic planning occurs when you work forward and backward simultaneously, adjusting and readjusting the work schedule as needed. When you are finished, your group will see the interconnections between all the people carrying out assignments. Don't rush the process. People need to feel comfortable both with the workload and the agreed-upon deadlines.

Depending on the scale of the plan you are facilitating, these five steps can all take place during one meeting, or they may occur over several meetings. In either case, it is crucial that you keep an accurate record of decisions made during the meeting so that a detailed summary of the proceedings can be generated and distributed to all parties soon afterward. This will help ensure that people follow through with their assigned tasks. The following are two examples of plans for different types of activities.

# Planning Format #1

**Event: Annual Banquet and Fundraiser**

**Committee Members:** Larry B., Ann C., Carmen, G., Stacey M., Chanice T., Kelly T., Suzanne M., Joy B.

**Date of Event:** April 12

**Meeting dates:** Nov. 15, Dec. 18, Jan. 18, Feb. 15, Mar. 15, Apr. 5, Apr. 11, Apr. 26

|  | November | December | January | February | March | April |
|---|---|---|---|---|---|---|
| **General** *(everyone)* | Determine theme<br><br>Generate list of possibilities for master of ceremonies, entertainment, and music | Develop list of potential donors for silent auction | Develop list of volunteers to assist with setup and cleanup on the day of the event | Review progress of silent auction solicitations | Review all logistics of event | Serve as host/hostess for event<br><br>Submit expense reports for reimbursement<br><br>Evaluate event |
| **Space, Food, Entertainment** *(LB, JB)* | Select banquet hall<br><br>Check availability of master of ceremonies, musicians, and entertainment | Sign contract for banquet hall<br><br>Make food selection<br><br>Sign contract with musicians, master of ceremonies, and entertainment | Determine AV needs with banquet hall<br><br>Make arrangement with adjacent parking lot for reduced parking fees for event | Purchase decorations<br><br>Order flowers<br><br>Order balloons | Finalize attendee numbers for food and drink order<br><br>Do final walk through with banquet hall manager<br><br>Confirm musicians and entertainment | Set up decorations and flower displays<br><br>Clean up after event<br><br>Send thank you notes to all volunteers |
| **Publicity** *(SM, AC, CM)* |  | Design invitation<br><br>Update database of names and addresses | Invitation to printer<br><br>Send press releases to media | Send out invitations<br><br>Send confirmation to attendees<br><br>Write draft of program<br><br>Schedule photographer | Proofread final program<br><br>Sent program to printer<br><br>Purchase thank you gifts for volunteers | Confirm photographer<br><br>Deliver programs to banquet hall<br><br>Select best photos, write press release for media and article for newsletter<br><br>Write thank you notes to master of ceremonies and volunteers |
| **Silent Auction** *(KT, CT, CG)* |  | Write draft of solicitation letter to donors, get approval by committee | Determine AV<br><br>Send letters to potential donors<br><br>Begin follow-up calls and personal visits to solicit donations for silent auction | Continue follow-up calls to potential donors<br><br>Write descriptions for program | Make display signs for auction items<br><br>Make raffle baskets, label<br><br>Train cashiers on auction procedures | Set up all silent auction displays<br><br>Write thank you notes to all donors |

## Tasks and Timelines for Updating Parent Handbook

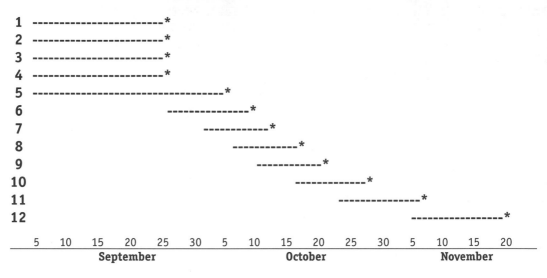

*denotes when task is completed

| Step | Tasks | Person Responsible |
|------|-------|--------------------|
| 1 | Update enrollment and personnel policies sections | Jake, Margie |
| 2 | Write overview of curriculum | Leticia |
| 3 | Update center philosophy section | Jake, Margie |
| 4 | Revise daily and annual schedule | Margie |
| 5 | Take photographs of children, staff, and facility | Ruby |
| 6 | Distribute to staff to review (discuss at Oct.10 staff meeting) | Margie |
| 7 | Submit to Parent Board for approval (Oct. 15 board meeting) | Margie |
| 8 | Incorporate revisions | Margie |
| 9 | Send to graphic designer for layout | Margie |
| 10 | Proofread final copy | Jake, Margie, Leticia |
| 11 | Take to printer | Jake |
| 12 | Distribute to staff, parents, and board | Margie |

## Problem-Solving Tools

The ability to use a systematic approach to problem solving is absolutely essential if you are to be effective in your role as a meeting facilitator. A problem is simply the gap between what is desired and what currently exists. But finding the solution to a complex problem can be a messy process. Effective facilitators know how to help a group identify and define the parameters of the problem, generate possible alternatives or solutions to the problem, evaluate and narrow those options, and decide on an appropriate course of action.

The key is to keep members focused on the same step of the process at the same time. Just how much time you spend on a particular problem depends on how important or trivial the issue is to the members of the group. Keep these four steps in mind the next time your group needs to tackle a thorny issue.

**Step 1. Define the problem.** Developing a clear definition of the problem that everybody agrees upon is essential if a viable resolution to the problem is to be found. This sounds so basic, but it is the step that is often neglected in the problem-solving process. The temptation for groups is to jump right into generating and evaluating solutions. Coming to agreement about the nature and scope of a problem is difficult because people have different perceptions of the issues they confront. One person's view may be a little or a lot different from someone else's view of the same situation.

The group's initial attempts at defining a problem will often be vague. They will most often describe the symptoms of the problem rather than zero in on the core problem itself. For example, teachers may complain that outdoor play time is a problem—too much wild and out-of-control behavior on the part of the children. As the discussion unfolds, however, you may find that the children's behavior is only a symptom of the problem. The real problem may be the design and layout of the outdoor play space, insufficient and inappropriate toys and equipment, or a lack of knowledge on the part of the teachers about how to engage children in constructive outdoor activities.

It is important during this first stage of the problem-solving process that you provide participants with a broader perspective of the issue than just their own. To do this, conduct a round-robin sharing where each person completes the following three statements:

- This is how I see the problem...

- I think the problem is the result of...

- This is how the problem has affected me so far...

**50%** of the solution of the problem comes in defining it.

Another technique you can use to help members more clearly define the problem is to ask each person to state what they believe to be the problem. In response to whatever the individual shares, you then ask, "Why is that a problem?" Allow him or her to answer the question, and then respond one more time with, "Why is that a problem?" This probing technique is useful for helping people "peel back the layers" and reveal their real concerns and the source of the problem.

Whichever technique you use to clarify the problem, make sure you also provide an opportunity for people to describe their ideal. The gap between one's ideal and current reality becomes the space for generating creative solutions. If the next phase of the problem-solving process is to be productive, you'll want to make sure that participants understand each other's vision of the ideal. You can't construct a bridge unless you know how deep and wide the valley is between the bank you're on and the bank you want to reach.

**Step 2. Generate alternatives.** Once the group has honed in and reached agreement on defining the problem, you are ready to guide them in generating alternatives for solving the problem. Brainstorming is perhaps the most widely used technique for getting the creative juices flowing and helping people make the shift in thinking needed to generate original ideas. The goal of brainstorming is to come up with as many different "rough-draft" ideas as possible in a short period of time, while suspending the urge to evaluate or come to agreement about a solution.

Brainstorming is a good technique to use when participants have sufficient background knowledge about the topic. For example, in the playground behavior problem scenario noted earlier, every teacher at the center could come up with one or two ideas of how the problem might be solved based on his or her experience working at the center. The power of brainstorming, though, comes in the synergistic effect of all staff working together to generate new solutions that no one thought of before.

Because the goal of brainstorming is to generate a lot of ideas, open acceptance of *all* ideas is essential. In typical meetings it is not uncommon for people who think quickly out loud to jump in and start sharing their ideas. Others in the group who may have a more reflective style or who are hesitant to speak up often don't get a chance to share their good ideas. As soon as someone speaks, everyone else is influenced to some degree by that person's contributions.

What happens is that people start elaborating and evaluating on the first few suggestions made rather than exploring new and completely different ideas. The number of ideas is thus limited. To prevent this from happening, ask participants to do some silent brainstorming first, writing down one or two ideas on a piece of paper before sharing their ideas with the whole group. This increases both the quantity and quality of the group's suggestions.

Questions that begin with *why, how*, or *what* lend themselves best to brainstorming. How can we decrease traffic congestion at dismissal time? What are some ways we can increase parent participation on field trips? As facilitator, your job is to keep the energy high, keep the ideas flowing, and keep people from evaluating the merits of the ideas proposed until the last suggestion has been tendered. Brainstorming works best in relatively small groups of 8-10 participants and when a climate of risk-taking exists so people feel free to toss out even wacky, weird, or outrageous ideas. In situations where many ideas will be generated, it may be productive to set a time limit. This brings energy to the group, limits analyzing ideas, and encourages uninhibited thoughts.

Recording all ideas on flip chart paper and posting them for everyone to see during the brainstorming session encourages people to "hitchhike," building upon other's ideas. Openly encourage people to modify, magnify, combine, or build off ideas that have been presented to come up with new ideas, but resist the temptation to start evaluating each contribution until all possibilities have been recorded. If there are a few individuals in the group who you feel might dominate the process, you may want to use a round-robin approach. If participation is fairly even, you can use a "popcorn" approach where people toss out ideas as they think of them.

## A Few Facilitator Tips to Encourage Brainstorming

### Do . . .

- keep things rolling at a fast clip.
- encourage people to take turns.
- treat silly ideas the same as serious ideas.
- move around to create a lively feeling.
- reiterate the purpose often: "Who else has a suggestion for increasing parent attendance at our annual fundraiser?"
- expect a second wave of creative ideas after the obvious ones are exhausted.

### Don't . . .

- interrupt when someone is offering an idea.
- say "We've already got that one."
- say "Hey, you don't really want me to write that one down, do you?"
- favor the "best" thinkers.
- use frowns, raised eyebrows, or other nonverbal language to signal skepticism.
- start the process without clearly setting the time limit.
- rush or pressure the group. Silence usually means people are thinking.

Adapted from Kaner, S. (1996). *Facilitator's guide to participatory decision-making* (p. 101). Gabriola Island, British Columbia: New Society Publishers.

**Step 3. Evaluate and narrow options.** There are essentially two ways to approach the task of evaluating and narrowing options. You can lead the group through a straightforward balance-sheet appraisal of each option presented, noting advantages and disadvantages and assessing the feasibility of the option. Or you can first develop a set of criteria with which to evaluate the options, and then assess each option based on the predetermined criteria.

The first approach can be quick and efficient if the issue is not too complicated or too controversial. Simply post sheets of flip chart paper on the wall, one per option, and in two columns note the pros and cons of each option. This approach is good because it forces people to talk about the positive aspects of each option rather than focusing only on the flaws of the ideas presented. The goal of using this balance-sheet approach is to help the group organize the information about potential options in such a way that the group is able to move to the next step of making an informed decision.

The alternative approach of first developing criteria with which to evaluate each option that is recommended if you think the group has the potential to become polarized around different positions. It is much easier to reach consensus about criteria before alternatives are discussed than afterward.

Criteria are essentially those things you hope to achieve, to maintain, or to avoid. They may have to do with feasibility, affordability, time, resources, desired outcomes, or any number of things the group deems important. It is best, however, to place a cap at four criteria or the evaluation process becomes too complicated. For example, if you were facilitating a group evaluation of alternatives to increase enrollment at your center, one of the criteria might be that the strategy be implemented with existing resources, or that the strategy also serve to expand community awareness of the program.

Most decisions in life are made by testing alternatives against personal criteria and selecting the one that best conforms. Working together as a group to develop criteria forces the group to externalize their values and share their inner decision-making assumptions. Such an exercise can provide rich insight and interpersonal awareness about why people favor one course of action over another. The down side of this approach is that it can be time consuming. Any discussion about criteria also raises the question about the relative importance of different criteria.

Once you have determined the appropriate criteria with which to evaluate your alternatives and have determined values to weigh the criteria, you are ready to move to the next step—prioritizing items. You can do this using a numerical scale or simply a low, moderate, high scale. For example, if you are evaluating staff recruitment strategies (creative want ads, contacting local colleges, using parents and current staff, financial incentives), the group could rank them according to cost-benefit criteria they developed.

**Problem:** The number of applicants for teaching positions at our center has decreased over the past two years. It has become increasingly difficult to attract qualified candidates.

**Reasons for the problem:**
1. Starting salaries and fringe benefits at our center are not as attractive as other job options in the community.
2. Six new centers have opened in the greater metro area during the past 18 months, making the competition for teachers even greater.
3. The number of early childhood students entering and graduating from the two local community colleges has decreased during the past three years.

**Resources to solve the problem:** Proceeds from annual fundraiser. This is $40,000 for the coming fiscal year.

**Question:** What strategy should we use to attract a larger pool of qualified teacher candidates?

**Criteria for evaluating alternatives:** The solution should...
1. Be easy to implement with existing administrative staff
2. Increase commitment to the center among new and continuing staff
3. Promote professionalism among new and continuing staff

| Alternatives | Criteria | | |
| --- | --- | --- | --- |
| | Easy to implement | Increase commitment | Promote professionalism |
| **Offer better benefits:** Staff would receive dental insurance coverage, a retirement plan contribution, or reduced tuition for child care. | M | M | L |
| **Increase base salaries:** For the coming fiscal year this would be an increase of $1.25 per hour for assistant teachers and $1.00 per hour for teachers. | M | H | M |
| **Expand recruitment strategies:** Place more ads in newspapers, distribute flyers at early childhood conferences, post ads at local colleges, provide bonuses to staff who refer candidates. | M | L | L |
| **Expand opportunities for professional development:** Pay travel and registration fee to two conferences, provide tuition reimbursement for college classes. | M | M | H |

Scale used for applying criteria: low, medium, high

**Step 4. Decide on a course of action.** You have arrived at the point when the group is ready to select the best solution from among several options. If you haven't rushed the previous steps, individuals at this point should be clear about the scope of the problem, appreciate how others feel about the problem, and understand the criteria used to evaluate alternatives to solve the problem. Certainly, there are faster ways to make decisions in groups. But if your goal is to elicit broad support for the decision, then investing time to follow this four-step problem-solving process is worthwhile.

If your group has used a criterion matrix to evaluate and narrow options, deciding on a course of action may be as straightforward as tallying responses to pinpoint the proposed solution that best meets the criteria. In some cases the decision won't be clear cut and you'll need to drop options with low ratings and reconsider those that remain again. If you used a balance-sheet approach to evaluate options, then you'll need to select from a variety of other consensus decision-making tools to help your group reach a final decision.

## Decision-Making Tools

Facilitators who embrace inclusive and participative approaches employ consensus decision making whenever possible. Unlike a majority vote, which forces participants into either/or positions and may result in gloating winners and resentful losers, consensus decision making allows participants in a meeting to express the degree to which they support a decision. While a majority vote may seem democratic, it can actually undermine group commitment to the decision. The minority, if not satisfied with the final decision, can sabotage it to keep it from being implemented.

Consensus does not mean that everyone embraces the final decision with the same degree of enthusiasm, only that each person has been fully heard and agrees to support the decision. To achieve consensus, it may be necessary to dissect the elements of a decision, reworking, redefining, and reconceptualizing it if necessary to reach an accommodation that everyone can support. The following table on pages 87-88 includes several possibilities for helping your group achieve consensus.

Groups often take pride when they are able to make quick and deliberate decisions. But quickness in decision making is not always a good thing; it can sometimes squelch individuals' initiative to speak their mind at the risk of slowing down the group's breakneck speed. As facilitator, if you sense that the group is coming to premature closure on an issue, you may want to say something like "We've made a pretty quick decision on this issue. Before we affirm this decision and move on, is there anything we may have overlooked in our discussion?" This will help the group re-examine the process and consider whether the decision was too hasty.

- **Nominal Group Technique.** This consensus strategy maximizes participant input while minimizing group power struggles. Go around the group giving everyone an opportunity to rank their choices from a list of options provided. Note these rankings on a large piece of flip chart paper. While doing this, provide an opportunity for individuals to speak about why they have ranked the items the way they have, but do not allow people to engage in a debate or discussion about what is said. When everyone has had an opportunity to post their rankings, go around the group one more time, inviting people to change their rankings based on the information they may have heard from others in the group. When completed, tally the scores for each option. The one with the highest point value is the option selected.

| | Option A | Option B | Option C | Option D |
|---|---|---|---|---|
| Jane | 3 | 1 | 2 | 4 |
| Amanda | 2 | 3 | 1 | 4 |
| Roule | 3 | 2 | 1 | 4 |
| Armando | 4 | 1 | 2 | 3 |
| Kristy | 1 | 3 | 2 | 4 |
| Kal | 2 | 3 | 1 | 4 |
| Trudy | 4 | 1 | 3 | 3 |
| Jillian | 2 | 3 | 1 | 4 |
| Total | 21 | 17 | 13 | 30 |

- **Human graph.** If folks are ready for a stretch when you are ready to vote, accomplish both at the same time. Ask group members to create a human graph by positioning themselves along a continuum of support (weak to strong; strongly disagree to strongly agree; not important to very important) that has been posted on the wall.

- **Finger vote.** Ask people to indicate the degree of their support for an option by holding up the number of fingers that corresponds to the strength of their support for an option:

  - Five fingers:   Total agreement, best solution, complete support
  - Four fingers:   Agree, good solution, support
  - Three fingers:  Okay with me, willing to support
  - Two fingers:    Don't agree, not my choice, but I can live with it
  - One finger:     No way, let's think of an alternative

- **Three-dot voting.** Post the options generated from a group discussion on pieces of flip chart paper on the wall. Distribute three different colored dots to members of the group. Have people stick a colored dot on each option that corresponds to their evaluation of the idea. For example:

  - Green:   Terrific idea, let's pursue it
  - Yellow:  Promising idea, may need some tinkering
  - Red:     Lousy idea, not worth pursuing

- **Straws in a cup.** Write out each option on a separate slip of paper and spread them out on a table. Put a cup next to each option. Distribute five straws to everyone in the group and ask them to vote by placing their straws in the cups next to their favorite options. Half-votes are permitted and individuals may cast more than one straw vote for an option they like.

- **1-2-6.** Ask individuals to write down their solutions to a problem on separate slips of paper. Then have them pair up with another person, share their ideas, and agree on a solution. Combine three pairs and have each group share ideas and generate a single solution. Ideas from the six-member groups are then shared to generate a solution by the entire group.

- **Cards up.** If you have a number of decisions to make or several items to which you want to assess participants' reactions, this technique gives you an instant reading of everyone's stand on the issue. Distribute a set of five cards boldly numbered 1 through 5 to each member of the group. When a vote is needed, ask everyone to simply hold up the card with the number that reflects their feelings on the issue. The scale could be 1= strongly disagree to 5 = strongly agree or any other scale that suits the issue under consideration.

For additional facilitation strategies that promote consensus decision making, be sure to read *Circle of Influence: Implementing Shared Decision Making and Participative Management,* another book in the Director's Toolbox Management Series.

## CHAPTER 7

# A Final Word

In reading this book you've taken a bold step toward transforming your meetings from ho-hum gotta-do obligations to energizing events that people leave with a better awareness of themselves, a greater appreciation of others, and a deeper commitment to the important work they do. You've learned in these pages that making the most of meetings is really a frame of mind— a personal commitment to doing a better job every time you don that facilitator's hat.

If you view each meeting you conduct as an opportunity to build and refine your leadership and facilitation skills, you'll ask yourself questions like, "What went well? Where did I encounter obstacles? How could I avoid these in the future?" Self-awareness is the first step to self-improvement. This means knowing what makes you behave the way you do in different situations and being keenly aware of your underlying values, assumptions, beliefs, preferences, and biases.

Think of self-assessment like the commentary you watch on television after a professional football game. Every aspect of the game is rehashed in a meticulous analysis. Do your own instant replay of the meetings you conduct, applying the same kind of detailed analysis and commitment to self-improvement.

Face-to-face feedback from meeting participants is also essential if you want to broaden your perspective and really understand what it is like to be a participant at one of your meetings. A genuine "How did you feel about yesterday's meeting?" can elicit valuable information that will help you hone your craft and better understand how you come across to others. Don't be afraid to ask people how you can improve.

Ultimately, the most valuable feedback on your performance comes when you consider how successfully you met your goals. Did the meeting achieve the results you hoped it would? Looking at the outcomes of the meeting is the best way to isolate aspects of the meeting structure, processes, and culture that may need to be improved.

Take a few minutes now to complete Exercise 5, "Reflecting on My Facilitation Skills." It serves as a summary of the major points covered in this book about the facilitation behaviors that foster effective meeting dynamics. When you have completed the exercise, look carefully at the items where you indicated "seldom." These are the areas where you can target your facilitation-improvement efforts.

> Excellence is the gradual result of always wanting to do better.
>
> *Pat Riley*

# Reflecting on My Facilitation Skills

| Behavior | Seldom | Occasionally | Often |
|---|---|---|---|
| I suggest a procedure for handling each topic when I introduce it. | | | |
| I model attentive listening and encourage others to do so. | | | |
| I monitor the clock, keeping discussion of each topic within the time constraints noted on the agenda. | | | |
| I help the group distinguish between fact and opinion. | | | |
| I encourage all members to participant, even quiet and reticent ones. | | | |
| I refocus the group when irrelevant discussion goes on too long. | | | |
| I am tactful in cutting off individuals whose joking or personal stories threaten to sidetrack the discussion. | | | |
| I strive for clarity in communication, asking members to explain the reasoning that led them to a conclusion. | | | |
| I help the group reaffirm its outcomes when the direction of proceedings becomes confusing. | | | |
| I suggest resources to help the group stay on track and achieve its goals. | | | |
| I connect one person's comments to those made by other participants. | | | |
| I summarize the discussion and decisions reached on each topic before moving on to the next. | | | |
| I seek common ground when conflicting points of view are expressed. | | | |
| I use humor to reduce the tension in the group when it is appropriate. | | | |
| I foster interpersonal connections that help people develop mutual respect and consideration. | | | |
| I provide an opportunity for participants to assess the effectiveness of the meeting at its conclusion. | | | |

As you adopt and adapt some of the strategies you've read in these pages, think about the facilitation style you want to cultivate. How you combine, modify, and personalize strategies to fit your personality and the context of your work situation will become your signature style as a facilitator. Skilled facilitators are able to combine strategies so that their leadership comes across as genuine and natural. Practice is the only way to achieve it.

Sometimes it is helpful to get the perspective of an outside observer. Such a person can provide an objective view of the group dynamic during your meetings. This person can also give you valuable feedback about the processes you use that may be helping or hindering your goal of leading a productive meeting.

A trained observer should be knowledgeable about group dynamics and the ingredients of effective meeting facilitation. Don't rely on a personal friend to do the job. You want someone who can give objective, candid, and useful feedback without worrying about jeopardizing your friendship if the news is not all good.

Remember, however, that the presence of an observer sitting in the back of the room taking notes during your meeting will probably have an impact on the group dynamic. People often exhibit "party behavior" when they know they are being observed, and you may feel stiff and awkward knowing that your every word and movement is being scrutinized. Even so, if you can overcome this self-consciousness and create a natural setting for an objective observation, the data you get will be invaluable in helping you polish your leadership facilitation skills.

In the end, meeting facilitation is an art, not a predictable science or pat formula to be followed. Skilled facilitators do have one thing in common, however—an attitude of experimentation and risk taking. They're not afraid to try new strategies, risk looking inept, or admit when they've made a mistake. Practice, careful observation of what works and what doesn't, and belief in your capacity to keep getting better is all it takes. With improved meeting skills come improved team effectiveness and more productive group outcomes. The payoff is definitely worth the investment. Good luck!

# For Further Reading

Barlow, C., Blythe, J., & Edmonds, M. (1999). *A handbook of interactive exercises for groups.* Boston: Allyn & Bacon.

Bendaly, L. (1997). *Strength in numbers.* New York: McGraw-Hill Ryerson.

Bloom, P. J. (2000). *Circle of influence: Implementing shared decision making and participative management.* Lake Forest, IL: New Horizons.

Bloom, P. J. (2000). *Workshop essentials: Planning and presenting dynamic workshops.* Lake Forest, IL: New Horizons.

Bloom, P. J., Sheerer, M., & Britz, J. (1991). *Blueprint for action: Achieving center-based change through staff development.* Lake Forest, IL: New Horizons.

Carter, M., & Curtis, D. (1998). *Visionary director: A handbook for dreaming, organizing, and improvising in your center.* St. Paul, MN: Redleaf.

The Center for Early Childhood Leadership. (2002, Winter). Factors impacting meeting productivity: Directors' and teachers' perceptions. *Research Notes.* Wheeling, IL: The Center for Early Childhood Leadership, National-Louis University.

Diamondstone, J. M. (1980). *Designing, leading, and evaluating workshops for teachers and parents.* Ypsilanti, MI: High/Scope Educational Research Foundation.

Doyle, M., & Straus, D. (1976). *How to make meetings work.* New York: Berkley.

Ettinger, J. (1989). *The winning trainer.* Houston, TX: Gulf.

Feigelson, S. (1998). *Energize your meetings with laughter.* Alexandria, VA: Association for Supervision and Curriculum Development.

Garmston, R. J., & Wellman, B. M. (1999). *The adaptive school.* Norwood, MA: Christopher-Gordon.

Hackett, D., & Martin, C. (1993). *Facilitation skills for team leaders.* Menlo Park, CA: Crisp.

Hamann, J. A. (1984). *How to avoid BORED meetings.* Madison: University of Wisconsin Press.

Harrington-Mackin, D. (1994). *The team-building toolkit.* New York: American Management Association.

Herbert, E., (1999, November). Rugtime for teachers: Reinventing the faculty meeting. *Phi Delta Kappan,* 219-22.

Haynes, M. E. (1988). *Effective meeting skills*. Menlo Park, CA: Crisp.

Hirsh, S., Delehant, A., & Sparks, S. (1994). *Keys to successful meetings*. Oxford, OH: National Staff Development Council.

Huszczo, G. (1996). *Tools for team excellence*. Palo Alto, CA: Davies-Black.

Janis, I. L. (1982). *Groupthink*. Boston: Houghton Mifflin.

Kaner, S. (1996). *Facilitator's guide to participative decision-making*. Gabriola Island, BC, Canada: New Society.

Kelsey, D., & Plumb, P. (1999). *Great meetings!* Portland, Maine: Hanson Park.

Kostelnik, M. J. (1984, August). Real consensus or groupthink? *Child Care Information Exchange*, 25-30.

Morrison, E. K. (1994). *Leadership skills: Developing volunteers for organizational success*. Tucson, AZ: Fisher.

Meservey, L., & Grundleger, G. (1992, September). Taking a new direction in staff meetings. *Child Care Information Exchange*, 55-57.

Neugebauer, B. (2000, November). Creating community, generating hope, connecting future and past: The role of rituals in our lives. *Child Care Information Exchange*, 48-51.

Neugebauer, R. (1982, July). Managing meetings. *Child Care Information Exchange*, 17-24.

Schwarz, R. M. (1994). *The skilled facilitator*. San Francisco, CA: Jossey-Bass.

Scott, J., & Flanigan, E. (1996). *Achieving consensus*. Menlo Park, CA: Crisp Publications.

Smith, K. K., & Berg, D. (1987). *The paradoxes of group life*. San Francisco: Jossey-Bass.

Schmuck, R. A., & Runckel, P. J. (1985). *The handbook of organization development in schools*. Palo Alto, CA: Mayfield.

Scholtes, P., Bayless, D., Massaro, G., & Roche, N. (1994). *The team handbook for educators*. Madison, WI: Joiner Associates.

Silberman, M. (1999). *One hundred and one ways to make meetings active*. San Francisco: Jossey-Bass/Pfeiffer.

Streibel, B. (1992). *Running effective meetings*. Madison, WI: Joiner Associates.

# APPENDICES

## Appendix A
Action Minutes

## Appendix B
Meeting Evaluation

## Appendix C
Checklist for Effective Staff Meetings

## Appendix D
Contributing to Meeting Productivity:
What Role Do I Play?

## Action Minutes

Members present: _____     Meeting Name: _____

_____     Meeting Date: _____

_____     Recorder: _____

| Agenda item | Summary of discussion | Decisions made | Tasks to be completed | Person responsible and due date |
|---|---|---|---|---|
| 1. | | | | |
| 2. | | | | |
| 3. | | | | |
| 4. | | | | |
| 5. | | | | |

| Next meeting | Possible agenda items |
|---|---|
| Date: _____ | 1. |
| Time: _____ | |
| Place: _____ | 2. |
| Things to bring: _____ | 3. |
| _____ | |
| _____ | 4. |

## Meeting Evaluation

Please take a few minutes to evaluate our meeting today. Circle the numeral for each criterion that best reflects your perceptions of the meeting.

**Agenda**
0    1    2    3    4    5
*Poorly constructed*     *Well constructed*

**Participation**
0    1    2    3    4    5
*Dominated by a few*     *Balanced among many*

**Listening**
0    1    2    3    4    5
*Inattentive*     *Attentive*

**Climate**
0    1    2    3    4    5
*Distrustful*     *Supportive, encouraging*

**Decisions**
0    1    2    3    4    5
*Forced by a few*     *Supported by all*

**Candor**
0    1    2    3    4    5
*Guarded*     *Open and direct*

**Use of Time**
0    1    2    3    4    5
*Poor*     *Efficient*

**Facilitation**
0    1    2    3    4    5
*Improvement needed*     *Effective*

**Creativity**
0    1    2    3    4    5
*Status quo reinforced*     *New ideas explored*

**Overall Meeting**
0    1    2    3    4    5
*Poor*     *Excellent*

*Other comments, observations, or recommendations:*

## Checklist for Effective Staff Meetings

|  | yes | no |
|---|---|---|
| 1. Were all participants informed ahead of time with a written agenda? | _____ | _____ |
| 2. Did the meeting start on time? | _____ | _____ |
| 3. Did the meeting begin on a positive note? | _____ | _____ |
| 4. Was the room arranged to facilitate interaction between members? | _____ | _____ |
| 5. Was the content of the meeting relevant to all participants? | _____ | _____ |
| 6. Did the group have enough background, information, and expertise to make necessary decisions? | _____ | _____ |
| 7. Did all participants have a chance to express their opinions and offer suggestions if they wanted to? | _____ | _____ |
| 8. Was the facilitator successful in keeping the discussion focused and on track? | _____ | _____ |
| 9. Did the facilitator restate and summarize issues when necessary? | _____ | _____ |
| 10. Was an understanding or consensus achieved on one issue before moving on to the next issue? | _____ | _____ |
| 11. Was there sufficient time allotted for each item? | _____ | _____ |
| 12. Did the facilitator allow enough room and flexibility to adapt the agenda to the needs of the group? | _____ | _____ |
| 13. Was the facilitator able to guide discussion so that it did not get bogged down in trivia or turn to petty gossip? | _____ | _____ |
| 14. Did participants listen respectfully to each other? | _____ | _____ |
| 15. Did most participants express themselves openly, honestly, and directly? | _____ | _____ |
| 16. Were differences of opinion on issues openly explored and constructively managed? | _____ | _____ |
| 17. When a decision was made, was it clear who would carry it out and when? | _____ | _____ |
| 18. Did the meeting end on a positive note? | _____ | _____ |
| 19. Did the meeting end on time? | _____ | _____ |
| 20. Overall, do you feel your time was well spent at this meeting? | _____ | _____ |

Do you have any suggestions for improving our meetings in the future?

# Contributing to Meeting Productivity: What Role Do I Play?

This assessment is designed to help you reflect on the actions and behaviors that contribute to productive meetings.  Please take a few minutes to read through the descriptors and indicate in the space provided if the behavior is one you exhibit in our group meetings *rarely, occasionally,* or *frequently*.  After you have reflected on your own meeting behavior, think about the other members of our work group.  In the space marked *others*, write the initials of one of your team members who you perceive regularly fulfills this function.

| | Rarely | Occasionally | Frequently | Others |
|---|---|---|---|---|
| **Initiating Ideas**<br>Presents new ideas for the group to consider. Helps define problems, suggests procedures, and proposes different tasks for the group to take on. | | | | |
| **Seeking Information**<br>Solicits information or opinions from group members and outside experts on different issues. Gathers facts and data for the group to use in its deliberations. | | | | |
| **Providing Information**<br>Offers facts and relevant information during group deliberations. Shares own experience and expresses opinions on different topics that are being discussed. | | | | |
| **Clarifying and Elaborating**<br>Seeks to clear up confusion regarding pertinent facts that have been presented. Defines jargon or acronyms for newcomers.  Paraphrases, amplifies, or interprets what has been said. | | | | |
| **Summarizing**<br>Restates key ideas that have been presented and summarizes what the group has covered. Makes connections between ideas expressed and suggestions for action. | | | | |
| **Evaluating**<br>Weighs proposals offered by the group against criteria for effectiveness or standards of quality. Assesses whether ideas offered are reasonable, practical, or doable. | | | | |
| **Testing for Closure**<br>Checks to see if the group is ready to make a decision, if it has reached consensus on an issue, or if it has completed discussion on a topic and is ready to move on. | | | | |
| **Encouraging**<br>Listens attentively, showing nonverbal and verbal approval of other members in the group. Is friendly, warm, and responsive to others and accepting of their contributions and opinions. | | | | |
| **Harmonizing**<br>Attempts to reconcile differing points of view. Looks for middle ground. Relieves tension so group members can explore differences productively. Senses and comments on the mood of the group. | | | | |
| **Gatekeeping**<br>Checks the flow of conversation to ensure that all members have a chance to speak.  Relates the relevance of topics discussed to all members rather than restricting discussion to only a few. | | | | |

# NOTES

# Available from New Horizons

## The Director's Toolbox:  A Management Series for Early Childhood Administrators

- *Circle of Influence: Implementing Shared Decision Making and Participative Management* $14.95

- *Making the Most of Meetings: A Practical Guide*  $14.95

- *The Right Fit: Recruiting, Selecting, and Orienting Staff*  $14.95 (available June 2002)

A Trainer's Guide is also available for each topic in the Director's Toolbox Series.  Each guide provides step-by-step instructions for planning and presenting a dynamic and informative six-hour workshop. Included are trainers' notes and presentation tips, instructions for conducting learning activities, reproducible handouts, and transparencies.  $69.95

## Other books by Paula Jorde Bloom

- *Avoiding Burnout: Strategies for Managing Time, Space, and People in Early Childhood Education*  $14.95

- *A Great Place to Work: Improving Conditions for Staff in Young Children's Programs*  $6.00

- *Blueprint for Action: Achieving Center-Based Change Through Staff Development*  $28.95

- *Blueprint for Action: Assessment Tools Packet*  $11.95

- *Workshop Essentials: A Guide to Planning and Presenting Dynamic Workshops*  $24.95

To place your order or receive additional information on quantity discounts, contact:

## NEW HORIZONS
P.O. Box 863
Lake Forest, Illinois 60045-0863
(847) 295-8131
(847) 295-2968 FAX